A Quest for Global Peace

A Quest for Global Peace

Rotblat and Ikeda on War, Ethics, and the Nuclear Threat

Joseph Rotblat and
Daisaku Ikeda

I.B. TAURIS
LONDON · NEW YORK

Published in 2007 by I.B.Tauris & Co Ltd
6 Salem Road, London W2 4BU
175 Fifth Avenue, New York NY 10010
www.ibtauris.com

In the United States of America and Canada
distributed by Palgrave Macmillan a division of St Martin's Press
175 Fifth Avenue, New York NY 10010

Hbk ISBN: 978 1 84511 278 3
Pbk ISBN: 978 1 84511 279 0

A full CIP record for this book is available from the British Library
A full CIP record is available from the Library of Congress

Library of Congress Catalog Card Number: available

Typeset in Palatino by JCS Publishing Services
Printed and bound in Great Britain by TJ International, Padstow, Cornwall

Contents

List of Illustrations

Foreword

by Robert Hinde

Joseph Rotblat and Daisaku Ikeda are not only great thinkers: they have spent their lives working for a peaceful world, a world in which all individuals would realize their full potential for the common good of humankind. This discourse between them is deeply moving and will be an inspiration to many.

Daisaku Ikeda is president of Soka Gakkai International, a non-governmental organization cooperating with the United Nations and dedicated to the realization of the universal values of human dignity and peace. As a Buddhist, Ikeda believes that all individuals possess the ability to create limitless value in harmony with others. Ikeda has devoted his life to the development of Soka Gakkai, and to the realization of a world in which the dignity and fundamental rights of all people are respected. He has founded numerous educational, peace and cultural institutions in many countries while maintaining an impressive literary output.

Joseph Rotblat, a scientist who believes in science as the way to solve humankind's problems, sees a role for religion, but is himself an agnostic. He helped to make the first atomic weapons because he believed that their possession by the Allies would prevent their use by either side, and was the only scientist to leave the project as a matter of conscience as soon as it became apparent that the Germans had abandoned their own attempts to make one. Horrified when he heard that atomic bombs had not only been used, but used against densely populated cities, Rotblat devoted his life to the abolition of nuclear weapons and to research in radiation medicine. Inevitably, both men focus on the need to abolish war, and are convinced that that is a real possibility. Both see education as an essential tool in achieving that goal.

Among Ikeda's numerous awards is the United Nations Peace Award. Rotblat has been the driving force in the Pugwash Conferences on Science and World Affairs. Pugwash is an organization which, operating out of the public eye, persuaded governments not to use nuclear weapons during the

Cold War and has continued to work for peace since the Cold War ended. Rotblat shared the Nobel Peace Prize with the Pugwash organization in 1995.

One wonders whether the ability of these two men to put ideals into practice sprang from the terrible circumstances they experienced in their youths. Rotblat nearly starved in Warsaw in Word War I; Ikeda experienced Japan's devastation in World War II. Or does it come from the influence of inspiring mentors in their late teens? In Rotblat's case this was Dr. Wertenstein, the Director of the Warsaw Radiological Laboratory, whom he saw as not only a first-rate scientist but also as a dedicated humanist who imparted the importance of ethical values; for Ikeda it was Josei Toda, the second president of Soka Gakkai, who published his Declaration Against Nuclear Weapons in the same year as the first Pugwash Conference.

It is highly significant that, though a generation apart, from different cultures and with differing philosophical orientations, they should agree so closely in so many ways, and especially in their emphasis on the need for basic human values. Central to their discussions, which include much material on the Manhattan Project and on the history of the Pugwash organization, is the need to create a peaceful world, a world in which all individuals could live in mutual understanding. Both seek some form of world governance in which local cultures will maintain their integrity, but cultural, ethnic and religious differences will not be a barrier to cooperation and friendship. Neither sees this as happening in the immediate future, and they emphasize the necessity to help the youth of today to find their proper role in life. In this, education must play a crucial role—not just the acquisition of facts, but education leading to learning and wisdom. Both agree on the importance of supporting the United Nations and respect for international law. Rotblat sees the future in the proper use of science, Ikeda in Buddhist philosophy and discourse, but this does not hinder a deep understanding between them, an understanding that arose from their common values and led to a close friendship.

Thus I am convinced that members of my generation, who experienced war, will find this book as moving as I did and, more importantly, that it will be an inspiration to all ages to do their utmost to serve humanity.

Robert Hinde

Preface

by Joseph Rotblat

The world today is different from the world into which I was born. In my opinion, the dominating factor contributing to change has been science. I was five years old when World War I broke out. Because my formative years were spent in poverty and suffering, I developed a tremendous passion for science as the means to alleviate the miseries of life that I experienced every day: hunger, disease, squalor, ignorance and cruelty. Science was the dream that sustained me in those terrible years.

Now, looking back at this childhood dream, I am glad to note that much of it has come true. Infectious diseases that killed so many infants and children are things of the past. Improved techniques in agriculture have made it possible, in theory at least, to feed the world's population. Moreover, new technologies in factories and mines have removed much of the drudgery and have increased safety standards. Technologies also have made obtaining food, clothing and shelter less of a daily chore. Progress in communication and information has given more people access to cultural achievements.

Altogether, people are nowadays more healthy, more affluent, better educated and informed—thanks to science—and thus better equipped to live in peace with each other. Sadly, I also must note some negative consequences of the applications of science.

Firstly, the benefits of science are not enjoyed by all people to the same degree. Gaps have widened between industrialized and developing nations, and between the upper and lower strata within nations. Furthermore, to the better-off nations and the affluent strata within nations—not satisfied with their high standards of living—affluence has brought excessive consumption of energy and squandering of natural resources. Excesses are leading to a catastrophic degradation of the environment. Above all, the application of science and technology to the development and production of weapons of mass destruction has created a real threat to the continued existence of the human race.

To a very large extent, threats to the environment and to humanity's continued existence were due to the work of scientists. Particularly in the case of weapons, they did this not because of any credible requirement for defense. This excess, simply to satisfy inflated egos or to experience the intense exhilaration in exploring new scientific concepts, is an example of the prostitution of science. It is a terrible but justified indictment of members of a highly respected group in society.

That human society is capable of being led to the folly of its own destruction is exemplified by another gruesome deed of the twentieth century: the Holocaust. This genocide was executed with scientific precision, using a chemical invented by a scientist, and perpetrated by one of the most civilized of nations. Weapons of mass destruction and genocide demonstrate the lunacy to which our minds can descend, the depravity to which society can sink. What is so worrying is that such evils are still with us.

Despite the horrible chapters in human history, I still believe in the inherent goodness of humankind. This has been my basic philosophy since my youth, and all the events that I have mentioned—including personal tragedy—have not shaken this belief.

There are signs that we are learning from history and moving toward a war-free world. For example, France and Germany used to be mortal enemies, as were other members of the European Union. There are still disputes, but the members of the European Union have learned to solve their problems by peaceful means. The same is taking place on other continents. Slowly and painfully we are appreciating the folly of war and learning to talk to each other.

All the same, for the concept of a war-free world to become universally accepted, a process of education is required. We have to eradicate a culture that accepts war. We have to change the mind-set that seeks security for one's own nation in terms that spell insecurity to other people's nations. Education will require efforts in two directions: a new approach to security in terms of global security, and nurturing a new loyalty—loyalty to humanity.

Global security requires, first, the reduction of major risks to humanity by the elimination of weapons of mass destruction. It is important to make the ban universal. We must not gloss over the hypocrisy that allows some nations to modernize nuclear weapons and ensconce them in their military doctrines while urging abstinence on everyone else. We must resolve that any use of these weapons would be a crime against humanity, excoriated by a shared morality.

We live in a world community of ever-greater interdependence due largely to technical advances arising from scientific research. We all owe an obligation to society, but the responsibility weighs heavily on scientists because of the dominant role played by science in modern society. Science must regain the respect of the community for its integrity. It must recapture public trust in its pronouncements. Scientists must reveal a human face and show that it is possible to combine creativity with compassion and to allow the imagination to roam while remaining accountable for their deeds.

An ethical code of conduct for physicians has been in existence for nearly two and a half millennia, since the days of Hippocrates. The Hippocratic Oath taken by doctors became essential when the life of a patient was literally in the hands of the doctor. Nowadays, scientists have acquired a somewhat similar role in relation to humanity. One such pledge, the one adopted by Pugwash students, reads as follows:

> I promise to work for a better world, where science and technology are used in responsible ways. I will not use my education for any purpose intended to harm human beings or the environment. Throughout my career, I will consider the ethical implications of my work before I take any action. While the demands placed upon me may be great, I sign this declaration because I recognize that individual responsibility is the first step on the path to peace.

I am in my ninety-seventh year, and have worked for the abolition of nuclear weapons, and ultimately of war itself, for most of my life. Fifty years ago, I joined Albert Einstein, Bertrand Russell and eight other scientists in signing a manifesto warning of the dire consequences of nuclear war. This statement, the Russell–Einstein Manifesto, was Einstein's final public act. Now I am the only remaining signatory. Because of this, I feel it is my duty to carry the message forward. What Einstein and his contemporaries wrote fifty years ago—"We have to learn to think in a new way"—is as relevant today as it was then.

When I signed the Manifesto, I was the youngest signatory. This dialogue, *A Quest for Global Peace*, written in partnership with a man younger than I, addresses the same dilemma. Can we remember our shared humanity and forget our differences? Can we master the necessary arts of global security and loyalty to the human race? Together with Daisaku Ikeda, I use this forum as a means to bequeath my experiences and my convictions about the moral and responsible uses of science to the next generation.

Joseph Rotblat
London

Preface

by Daisaku Ikeda

> War turns people into mindless beasts ... People who detest barbarism start to act in barbaric ways. This is the insanity of war!

These were the unforgettable words spoken to me by Professor Joseph Rotblat, the distinguished scientist and peace activist. The occasion was our first meeting, in Osaka in 1989. As he spoke, his expression, usually mild as a spring breeze, took on a look of undisguised anger.

The Holocaust carried out by the Nazi regime brought him tragedy, taking his beloved wife from him. And though he resigned from the Manhattan Project while it was midway in its work of developing the atomic bomb, he was left with feelings of shame because he had participated in the production of the bomb. World War II inflicted wounds on his keen mind and spirit that could never be healed, and it marked the time from which his true struggle as a human being began.

He began his search for a kind of science that would not inflict destruction and slaughter but would contribute to human happiness. He became involved in researching for a cure for cancer, and at the same time he devoted himself to the movement for world peace. He worked to convert the greatest miseries of war into the most intense determination for peace, channeling all his energies into the movement to abolish nuclear weapons.

In 1957, the Pugwash Conferences, an international organization of scientists dedicated to the abolition of nuclear weapons, was founded, and with that as his springboard, Professor Rotblat devoted the remainder of his life to the cause of peace. Meanwhile, in the same year, 1957, in Japan my mentor, Mr. Josei Toda, the second president of the Soka Gakkai, declaring that nuclear weapons constituted "an absolute evil", called upon young people to work for their abolition. Though the two men never met, they were in perfect agreement in insisting that barren rivalries of political ideology be transcended and that the existence of nuclear weapons be outlawed.

In part, no doubt, because of this historical coincidence, Professor Rotblat responded warmly to SGI's (Soka Gakkai International's) popular-based peace movement and expressed his concurrence. As he himself said, "We share a common goal with you. The struggle for peace will no doubt take a lot of fighting, but from now on I hope we can work together to carry that fight forward."

In 1995 Professor Rotblat received the Nobel Peace Prize, and in the years following it seemed that he was busier than ever in his efforts for peace. I have no doubt that he was spurred to even greater activity by his sense of mission and responsibility because of the fact that, among those who signed the momentous Russell–Einstein Manifesto of 1955, he was the last surviving member.

When Professor Rotblat and I met a second time, in Okinawa in 2000, I could see that he was working harder than ever to achieve his goal. "I can't afford to be tired!" he remarked when I asked how he was bearing up. Professor Rotblat and I began exchanging letters when he expressed a strong desire to appeal to the young people of the next generation to carry on the ideals of the Russell–Einstein Manifesto. How the torch of peace could best be transmitted to the younger generation was one of the deepest concerns of his later years, and he became increasingly concerned with educating the young in this respect.

In this connection he kindly agreed to visit Soka University of America, which I founded in California, and to deliver a lecture there. It was in October of 2001, when America was still in turmoil from the 9/11 terrorist attacks. Professor Rotblat, fatigued by the long journey from his home in London, was in a state of exhaustion, and in the car carrying him from the airport to the campus, took doses of medication that he had brought with him. He was ninety-two at the time, but the fervent words he spoke in the lecture, straining his voice, deeply impressed the hearts and minds of the students with his personal manifesto of "the spirit of peace".

The book presented here is entitled *A Quest for Global Peace*. The title is intended as a tribute to Professor Rotblat's ardent battle for the realization of his ideals, and it sums up the theme of the lecture he gave at Soka University of America. Through the medium of these discussions with me, he said that he hoped to give full expression to his thoughts on the subject of peace and was untiring in his efforts to bring them to publishable form.

It was the first week of August of 2005 when we completed the final editing of our discussions—just sixty years from the event that marked the beginning of Professor Rotblat's efforts for peace, the dropping of atomic bombs on Hiroshima and Nagasaki. Not long after, Professor Rotblat's journey came to an end; he died peacefully in London on August 31 at the age of ninety-six. His life spanned a century of dramatic change and constituted a powerful drama of victory achieved.

Six years ago in Osaka, where we had had our first memorable encounter, I arranged to have two cherry trees planted in honor of Professor Rotblat and his wife. Viewing the trees this spring, I found them in full bloom, with a pink that called to mind the healthy glow of Professor Rotblat's cheeks.

The death of my mentor, Mr. Toda, took place at a similar time, in April when the cherries were at their best. I recall how he once said to me, speaking in a voice charged with emotion,

> War can never be done away with simply by modifying the social system or changing the structure of the nation. Only a change in the fundamental nature of the human being will do that. The people as a whole must become stronger. The people must become wiser. The people of the world must join together heart to heart - there is no other way!

These words of his echo the message that runs throughout the Russell–Einstein Manifesto, the injunction "Remember your humanity!" Next year will mark the fiftieth anniversary of the founding of the Pugwash Conferences and the issuance of Mr. Toda's Declaration Against Nuclear Weapons. It seems highly fitting, therefore, that this compilation of dialogues between Professor Rotblat and myself should appear in print on the eve of that anniversary. It constitutes, in effect, a posthumous work by Professor Rotblat, and because of its importance, is appearing simultaneously in both a Japanese and an English version.

My enduring hope is that the young people of today will be inspired by this book and by the example of Professor Rotblat's lifetime of devotion to come forward one after another and join in the unprecedented challenge which they present, namely, the creation of a world free of nuclear weapons and of war.

Daisaku Ikeda
President, Soka Gakkai International

CHAPTER 1

One World, One Table, One Will to Unring the Nuclear Bell: Pugwash

Ikeda: Professor Rotblat, I have had the opportunity to engage in dialogues with many of the world's leading peace advocates who have made great contributions to world peace. But I am particularly pleased to have the opportunity to speak with you. You are a man of courage and justice who, more than anyone in the twentieth century—a century of war and violence—has steadfastly summoned up all your strength in your struggle to bring about world peace.

I would like to encourage you, for the sake of future generations, to tell the story of your inspiring life as well as to share with us your philosophy. I believe that for humanity to transform the twenty-first century into a century of peace, your wisdom and vision are an essential guide. Let us begin our dialogue forthwith, with the goal of eradicating from the earth war and the tragedies it inflicts on humankind.

Rotblat: Dr. Ikeda, I have looked forward to this day for quite a while. I am deeply moved finally to be able to speak with you. You are an energetic man, much younger than I, and are well known around the world as a figure filled with the drive and determination to accomplish our goal. I am one of your greatest admirers. I consider you a world leader, a champion, as well as an ambassador for peace.

Commitment to peace and political will

Ikeda: You are very gracious, but let us focus on you, a lion of peace. I would like to mention the international conference held in February 2000 by the Toda Institute for Global Peace and Policy Research, which I founded, and to thank you again for rushing all the way to Okinawa to attend. On that occasion you were awarded the Toda Prize for Peace Research; what I will never forget is that you insisted in your speech on Japan's taking the lead in the abolition of nuclear weapons. You eloquently expressed the anger, bitterness, sorrow, and grief that you feel about the tragedy and destruction of war. At the same time, you voiced your firm conviction and desire to transform the world into a peaceful place. You warned that humanity faces the deepest crisis of its existence, and that we have no choice but to act.

At the conference in Okinawa, we affirmed our commitment to peace and pledged to continue our conversations for the benefit of future generations. I am so pleased that we have realized our wish.

Rotblat: Dr. Ikeda, I have a specific request to make of you. As you know, humankind is trapped in an extremely difficult predicament. Somehow, we must overcome this situation as soon as possible. I would like to ask you to exercise your global leadership to bring about a change in the situation necessary to ensure peace in the world. I believe that you have the capacity to make a significant impact.

Ikeda: I appreciate your profound understanding of the world's situation. You have my word that I will do my utmost for the sake of humanity. It seems that, since entering the twenty-first century, the visibility on the path toward a world without war and nuclear weapons has become foggier than ever. Professor Rotblat, you expressed a grave sense of alarm in a speech you gave on the occasion of the International Physicians for the Prevention of Nuclear War (IPPNW)/Physicians for Social Responsibility(PSR) Fifteenth World Congress in May 2002 entitled "The Nuclear Issue: Where Do We Go From Here?" You said, "The drive for the elimination of nuclear weapons is not going well; indeed, it is going very badly."

The topic of nuclear proliferation is given much attention, but people do not discuss the fundamental threat of power based on nuclear weapons itself. I do not sense that the nuclear powers have the political will to proceed immediately with nuclear disarmament and abolish nuclear weapons within a specified period of time. Rather, a pro-war sentiment seems to be growing, under the guise of increasing "security" and implementing "crisis management".

In reality, the historical record of the sixty years following the birth of the nuclear age is declared in the statement, "As long as nuclear weapons exist, they will spread." Since 1945, beginning with the Soviet Union in 1949, we have seen the progressive proliferation of nuclear weapons. And this is despite the existence of the Nuclear Non-Proliferation Treaty.

Certain countries openly possess nuclear weapons. Other countries see themselves as forbidden to possess them. In principle, this situation is unjust, unstable and ultimately unsustainable. Only two possibilities can result from this. Either nuclear weapons will spread to every country on earth, or all countries will agree to abolish them. The first possibility leads to the extinction of the human race. We have no choice but to choose the second option. Just because the choice is a difficult one does not mean that we can avoid dealing with it. We must have the courage to grapple with this issue and act on our convictions.

Rotblat: Yes, indeed. Our only salvation from extinction is to make choices that ensure the realization of a peaceful world. For many years security in the world was governed by the ancient Roman dictum, *Si vis pacem, para bellum* (If you wish for peace, prepare for war). Given the general acceptance of this conventional wisdom, the attitude of people these days is not surprising. However, as history tells us, it is an indisputable reality that preparations for war have generally led to war. Despite this, we have insisted on putting our faith in this premise.

If humanity hopes to survive into the third millennium, we must rewrite the ancient Roman dictum to read, *Si vis pacem, para pacem* (If you wish for peace, prepare for peace). Each of us is a member of the human family, and we enjoy our lives within this context. For this reason, we must never forget that we have a duty and responsibility to make sure that this human community endures.

Birth of the Pugwash Conferences: a businessman's generosity

Ikeda: You have assisted in the operations of the Pugwash Conferences on Science and World Affairs since their inception in 1957, and for many years have served as its secretary-general. During the Cold War, you poured all your energies into bringing together scientists from East and West for face-to-face discussions.

Beginning in 1988, as president of the Pugwash Conferences, you have played a leadership role in the movement to abolish nuclear weapons. In 1995, you were awarded the Nobel Peace Prize. Ever since, you have continued to be active, as president emeritus, in advocating world peace.

Professor Rotblat, you have been integrally involved in all the major contributions made by the Pugwash Conferences for over half a century, and
the organization's remarkable achievements all evolved from the very first
conference, held in a small Canadian fishing village. Isn't that right?

Rotblat: Yes. The Pugwash Conferences take their name from that small
fishing village. The reason that we met there is because of Cyrus Eaton, an
Ohio businessman who wrote to Lord Bertrand Russell. Eaton's letter
reached Russell just days after the announcement of the Russell–Einstein
Manifesto, and it conveyed the following proposal: "Could I help toward
the realization of your proposal by anonymously financing a meeting of the
scientists in your group at Pugwash, Nova Scotia? I have dedicated a com-
fortably equipped residence there by the sea to scholarly groups." At the
time, we did not give this proposal much thought.

Ikeda: At first, you didn't plan to hold a conference in Pugwash.

Rotblat: It was because, at that time, we were already pursuing plans to
hold the conference in India. Indian Prime Minister Jawaharlal Nehru was
enthusiastically encouraging us to hold the conference in New Delhi. However, the instability of the global situation in 1956 caused by the Hungarian
uprising and the Suez Canal crisis, which led to the closing of the canal,
forced us to cancel the conference in India, scheduled to be held in January
1957.

This was when I remembered the letter from Cyrus Eaton. I first had to
find out if his offer still stood, so I sent him a telegram, and fortunately
received an affirmative reply. The conference would be in Canada, and we
devoted ourselves anew to preparations.

Cyrus Eaton was born in the town of Pugwash. He not only offered his
residence for the conference, but also provided funding to cover the cost of
travel and other expenses for all the conference participants during their
stay in Pugwash. This was how, in July of 1957, we were able to hold a
conference with twenty-two scientists from ten countries around the world
attending, including those from the Eastern bloc countries like the USSR
and Poland.

Ikeda: Eaton provided the funding for the conference and promised not to
interfere in any way with the conference proceedings. Thanks to this sincere, concerned businessman, who longed for peace, a first step was taken
on the long journey toward creating a nuclear abolition movement.

Interestingly, in the same year as the first Pugwash Conference, my teacher and mentor Josei Toda, the second president of Soka Gakkai, announced his Declaration Against Nuclear Weapons, a year before his death. The significance of the Declaration was that, as a practicing Buddhist, my mentor acutely understood from the depths of his soul that nuclear weapons would become the greatest threat hanging over humankind. When I consider these common concerns, I cannot help but feel a profound bond with the Pugwash Conferences.

Pugwash and Japan

Rotblat: We were of like mind, and I regret that I was unable to meet Mr. Toda before he died. I believe that Soka Gakkai International (SGI), beginning with Josei Toda and continuing with you, Dr. Ikeda, and all the dedicated SGI members, have shared with the Pugwash Conferences the same goal of creating a world without war and nuclear weapons.

1. The participants of the first Pugwash Conference, 1957

Ikeda: Certainly, abolition of nuclear weapons is a common wish of thinking people in the world. But if we are unable to realize such a world, peace, in the true sense of the word, will remain elusive, and indeed, humanity's future itself will be in jeopardy. Incidentally, I believe that three Japanese scientists attended the first Pugwash Conference in Canada. Two of them, Hideki Yukawa and Shin'ichiro Tomonaga, were Nobel Laureates in Physics, and the other one was the physicist Iwao Ogawa. Professor Tomonaga, who helped with the preparations for the Canadian conference, shared his reflections on the event.

He said, "The very first Pugwash Conference was, of course, significant for the conclusions that were reached, but also important was the conviction that scientists from East and West could talk together. We learned from this experience that if we could speak frankly and amiably, no matter how different our beliefs, areas of agreement could be reached."[1]

Every day during the five-day conference, there were heated discussions among the scientists from morning to late at night. During the Cold War, the discussion of political issues such as military disarmament and peace must have been fraught with many difficulties.

Rotblat: Frankly, in the beginning we were concerned that the strained political relations created by the Cold War would lead to emotional confrontations with the Soviet scientists, who held such a different political perspective. As it turned out, however, the conference ended with unanimous agreement to establish a new organization that would allow the dialogue to continue. In this sense, as Professor Tomonaga pointed out, the conference became a significant historic encounter between scientists from the East and West.

When the twenty-two scientists met at Pugwash, no one predicted that this would be the start of a new global movement. Many feared that the conference would end in irreconcilable arguments. But on the contrary, the conference provided the opportunity for participants to establish long-lasting friendships. This was definitely true in my case. For example, I enjoyed meeting the three scientists from Japan and soon became good friends with them. Of these, Professor Ogawa was nearest to my age, and so we felt very close. After the conference, we corresponded and deepened our friendship.

Ikeda: That's wonderful. Professor Ogawa was professor of physics at Rikkyo University for many years and, I understand, was very sympathetic to our SGI peace movement activities.

From many years of experience, I can attest to the truth of Professor Tomonaga's statement that if scientists speak frankly and amiably, areas of agreement can be reached despite their differences. This belief was strengthened at the height of the Cold War when I visited the socialist countries, including the USSR and the People's Republic of China, to engage in dialogue with many political and academic leaders to forge a path for friendly relations.

In September 1974, on my first visit to the Soviet Union, I met with Premier Aleksei Kosygin. In our discussion we touched on the topic of food problems, and he told me succinctly, "We must first of all abandon the idea of waging war. War is meaningless. If people were able to prepare for peace rather than war, they could be growing food rather than making military armaments." I still vividly remember this thought.

Professor Rotblat, you were a co-chair of the Canada conference. To what do you attribute the success of the conference?

Recipe for success: personal respect and professional trust

Rotblat: Let's see. First of all, many of the scientists who attended the conference were participants in the Manhattan Project during World War II, and because they were nuclear weapons specialists, they knew full well the catastrophic consequences of nuclear weapons.

Also, all of the participants had played an active role in international affairs, and so they did not approach difficult issues with preconceived ideas. I believe that this was due largely to the fact that these were scientists, and their traditional training in the scientific method allowed them to respect facts and make impartial decisions. Also, as scientists, we were all familiar with each other's writings, which often meant that we had already developed personal relationships, and we respected each other as people as well as scholars. In spite of the fact that much of the discussion was of a political nature, through our propensity for rational analysis and objective inquiry, we deepened our appreciation and trust of one another.

As a result, the conference, which was planned as a single event, exceeded even our own expectations for success, and we determined to continue holding the conferences on a regular basis. A planning committee was appointed, and its first meeting was held in London.

Ethics of universality

Ikeda: This is a remarkable history. It is also apparent that this respect you had for one another as scientists formed a valuable foundation vital to the success of your discussions.

Norman Cousins is another figure who made an enormous contribution to furthering East–West relations during the Cold War. In my published dialogues with him, Mr. Cousins described his role in serving as US President John F. Kennedy's personal envoy to Moscow to meet with Premier Nikita Khrushchev. Mr. Cousins had an undying faith in the possibilities of the human heart, and most important of his convictions was the view that a true understanding of others comes about through mutual cooperation.

First of all, we must be amenable to talking together and cooperating with each other. This is the point at which we can transcend differences and open up a path toward mutual understanding. If we stubbornly insist on reaching an understanding before working together in collaborative relationships, then mutual understanding will be forever beyond our grasp. In my efforts to extend bridges of friendship in a divided and divisive world, the reason that I have especially dedicated my attention to establishing opportunities for educational exchange is that I feel strongly that the educational and scholarly spheres pulse with an ethic of universality and oneness of all people that transcends nationalism and ideological differences.

I mentioned previously my first visit to the Soviet Union. This trip took place during an especially tense period in Soviet–Chinese relations. I visited both China and the USSR because I felt particularly challenged to help resolve the strained relations.

When I visited the University of Moscow, I noticed a large picture prominently displayed on the front wall of the university president's office. It was a present from Peking University that depicted the grandeur of the University of Moscow. When I was told about the origin of the picture, I was convinced that the world of politics may be fraught with harsh conflict, but there are no national boundaries in the world of scholarship. I felt that it was inevitable that the Soviet Union and China would eventually develop a harmonious relationship. And indeed, history has proven this to be correct.

Opening the "Iron Curtain"

Rotblat: How interesting. I believe that our major role during the Cold War was to provide an opportunity for scientists, who had been estranged from one another because of the "Iron Curtain", to get together and talk with each other, not as representatives of countries or organizations, but as individuals. These informal relationships continued through the Vietnam War and the Afghanistan crisis, though US–Soviet relations were severely strained.

The Eastern bloc countries restricted freedom of thought and mobility, yet the Soviet Academy of Sciences felt that Soviet scientists should be of the same caliber as the Western scientists, and so it used its considerable influence to enable prominent Soviet scientists to represent the Soviet Union at the Pugwash Conferences. As a result, Lev Artsimovich, Nikolai

Bogolubov, and Peter Kapitza attended. These were scientists who had a major influence on national policy and who were not afraid to voice their thoughts, whether or not their views differed from their country's official policies.

Ikeda: You and your colleagues endured many years of criticism and slanderous attacks for sitting down at the table with scientists from the Eastern bloc. I also have been the target of baseless attacks for my visits to the Soviet Union and China. I have been asked why I, a religious person, would visit a country that denies religion.

As the central figure in the Pugwash Conferences, Professor Rotblat, you have toiled long and hard to bridge the gap between East and West. What was your most difficult experience in your work for the Pugwash Conferences?

Rotblat: As your comments intimate, for whatever reason, it was a time in which the mere mention of making the abolition of nuclear weapons a movement's objective was tantamount to being a tool of Soviet propaganda. Therefore, meeting with Soviet scientists and being heartened by the opportunity to discuss ways to bring about peace and military disarmament immediately branded one as a communist or communist sympathizer. I was severely criticized and called naive, a dupe, and easy prey to Soviet manipulation. In the midst of all this, I took the utmost care to conduct the running of the conference so as to maintain unimpeachable confidence from all the parties from both East and West.

Ikeda: You did a marvelous job. You reminded me of Professor Linus Pauling, who also devoted himself to the nuclear abolition movement and who, in a dialogue with me, reflected on those days. He said that most of the scientists refrained from speaking out in public, but, "perhaps out of stubbornness, I refused to allow McCarthy and the anticommunists in the United States to silence me."[2] Perhaps the two of you shared the same outlook.

Rotblat: Professor Pauling was a truly great man. I am sure that we, Professor Pauling and I, had many of the same convictions.

Getting back to your previous question, the Pugwash Conferences came to the first major crossroads in 1960 when the Soviet government invited us to send a representative from the Pugwash Conferences to Moscow to be a part of the planning for a world congress on disarmament. The reason was that, as might seem obvious, the Pugwash Conferences shared the same objective of military disarmament as the Soviet conference, which was to be held in Moscow. It seemed as if there was no justifiable reason not to collaborate.

Some of our members felt that we should accept the offer to participate in the conference, but I insisted that our participation would have signaled support for Soviet propaganda, and on that basis, the offer must be firmly refused. Ultimately, my view prevailed, and the Soviet invitation was declined.

Ikeda: You were confronted with numerous difficult circumstances, it seems.

Rotblat: Yes. I'll never forget when, after one debate, a member of the Soviet delegation unobtrusively took me aside and personally thanked me for opposing his proposal. Even though he was a member of the Communist Party, he recognized the importance of the Pugwash Conferences as an avenue of communication between East and West. Undoubtedly, he was secretly relieved that the Conferences were able to retain the trust of the Western bloc countries.

For years afterwards, the belief in the Western bloc countries was that the Pugwash Conferences represented a genuine effort toward peace.

Educating the public conscience

Ikeda: I am deeply moved that the Soviet scientists thanked you privately for your efforts. This is important historical evidence that you have shared. Overcoming political partisanship is more easily said than done. I am sure that this was even more the case in an era of sharp ideological conflict. It was the consciences of the individual participants from East and West that provided the underlying support for the Pugwash Conferences.

The Pugwash Conferences have made extraordinary efforts over many years. The third conference held in Vienna in September 1958 is a good example of the way the Pugwash Conferences seek to educate a wide audience on conference issues and conclusions. I have heard that the "Vienna Declaration", which highlighted the conclusions of the conferences, was announced to an auditorium of assembled citizens, including the President of Austria, who attended as an observer.

Rotblat: Yes. The conference was held on a grand scale, drawing over ten thousand people to the Vienna Municipal Hall to hear ten scientists, including Lord Bertrand Russell, speak. This was also the setting in which the Vienna Declaration was adopted. The Declaration articulated the principles and objectives of the Pugwash efforts, including the hope of abolishing not only all nuclear weapons, but also war itself. After the Declaration was announced, it was sent to scientists in many countries and was signed by thousands of sympathizers.

Ikeda: I am truly impressed with the Pugwash insistence that we must create a world without war, even as we strive for the abolition of nuclear weapons.

This is also the path that Soka Gakkai and SGI have followed. Incidentally, one of the crises that the Pugwash Conferences faced was how to handle the sudden resumption of nuclear tests by the Soviet Union just before the eighth Pugwash conference. This conference was held in the US in September 1961. Somehow, a total breakdown was avoided through the patience and wisdom of the conference organizers and participants, and the episode deepened the conviction that, as Professor Tomonaga wrote, "No matter what difficulties we faced, we were firmly convinced that it was possible as well as imperative that we continue our talks."

So it seems that this conference was the turning point that mobilized the organization to begin seriously searching for specific means to avoid a nuclear war.

Accepting the logic of arms reduction

Rotblat: That is correct. During the Cold War, when East–West enmity threatened to engulf the world in a "hot war", the main task of the Pugwash Conferences was to avert a major crisis. The aim was to avoid a nuclear war by any means and terminate the nuclear arms race that was responsible for the heightened tensions in the first place.

One specific means to ease tensions was to urge the conclusion of a treaty. For example, the Partial Nuclear Test Ban Treaty, which despite its many restrictions, was put into place and succeeded in slowing the speed of the arms race. However, a resolute return to activities to abolish nuclear weapons had to wait until the end of the Cold War.

Ikeda: Professor Rotblat, we first met in October 1989, just before the fall of the Berlin Wall, that monumental symbol of the Cold War. On that occasion, nuclear arms reduction was not progressing smoothly, and the cause, you pointed out, was that government leaders did not understand or accept the logic of arms reduction. You stressed the importance of vanquishing the fallacy of nuclear deterrence, because there is absolutely no way that nuclear arms would prevent a war.

I was deeply struck by your reflections on the tragedy of the two world wars. You warned, "War turns people into mindless beasts. Even scientists who are normally highly logical lose their rationality when a war breaks out. People who detest barbarism start to act in a barbaric way. This is the insanity of war."[3]

Rotblat: I came to Japan to attend a symposium held in Tokyo, just a year after I assumed the presidency of the Pugwash Conferences. On the same occasion, you paid us the highest compliment when you said, "The members of the Pugwash Conferences seek to save humankind by guiding it down the right path. There is no mission or work more honorable."

In 1993, we published a book, *A Nuclear-Weapon-Free World: Desirable? Feasible?*[4] in response to the hopes many people had for the Pugwash movement. We declared that a world without nuclear weapons was a world worth working for and presented a clear and concrete plan to realize this objective.

Ikeda: The Japanese edition, attracting great public attention, was published in 1995.

The major achievements of the Pugwash Conferences are: giving a voice to scientists of conscience, arousing international public opinion, and also earnestly searching for effective strategies to resolve the nuclear arms situation.

My mentor, Josei Toda, repeatedly emphasized the importance of presenting a clear and concrete plan for progressing toward peace for humanity. He stressed, "Even if the goal is not achieved immediately, ultimately, your efforts will serve as kindling, and the warm glow of peace will spread. Empty theories are useless, but a clear and concrete plan serves as a pillar supporting the structure that will protect humankind." Every year I deliver a Peace Proposal to the world, and my teacher's words have motivated and spurred me to search for a resolution to many global problems.

Rotblat: That is truly marvelous. I mentioned this when I met you in Okinawa five years ago, and I reiterate now, we humans are facing an extremely serious impasse. We must somehow extricate ourselves from this situation.

Dr. Ikeda, I am counting on you to take up the mantle of leadership. I believe that we have no choice but to entrust our future to leaders who are able to accomplish the ultimate goal.

Ikeda: As the disciple of Josei Toda, who sincerely hoped for the construction of a world without nuclear weapons and war, I am determined to respond to your kindness, Professor Rotblat, with actions rather than simply ideas.

I would like to continue to strive mightily together with you, distinguished professor, to create peace. I believe that only an enlightened populace can vanquish war, the ultimate evil, through justice and alliances with like-minded people.

CHAPTER 2

Hiroshima and Nagasaki:
From Japan's Ground Zero to the World

Ikeda: Hiroshima was chosen as the site for this summer's [2005] annual General Assembly of the Pugwash Conferences. Hiroshima is significant because it represents the beginning of the nuclear age—what Danish physicist Niels Bohr calls humankind's ground zero, a completely new situation that defies resolution by war.

We are anticipating that Hiroshima will send a strong message of peace to the world on the sixtieth anniversary of the dropping of the atomic bomb and fiftieth anniversary of the Russell–Einstein Manifesto.

Rotblat: I am deeply grateful that you grasp the immense significance of the Pugwash Conferences. Unfortunately, the Review Conference of the Nuclear Non-Proliferation Treaty, held in New York in May of this year [2005], ended, after intense debate, in failure to reach an agreement between the nuclear and non-nuclear powers.

Ikeda: The review conferences are held every five years with the objective of preventing the spread of nuclear weapons. The breakdown of the last conference is an alarming development because the current international environment begs a recognition of the complexity and evolving crisis surrounding nuclear issues.

Rotblat: Speaking as a long-time participant in the forum of nuclear weapons, I have a profound awareness of the importance of the Nuclear Non-Proliferation Treaty (NPT). The current crisis is the worst that I have seen in the entire history of the treaty. I strongly believe that as long as the nuclear powers do not make a good faith effort to undertake nuclear disarmament, the crisis of nuclear proliferation will not be diffused.

I sent a message to the recent NPT review conference. In my statement, I specifically urged conference participants to move beyond the outdated security system based on "nuclear deterrence" to a new system of collective security based on cooperation and the recognition of our common goal for human survival.

Ikeda: I am in complete agreement. If current trends continue, humankind's future will not be secure. The nuclear age requires a reorientation of our perceptions of "security". Our leaders must take a cold, hard look at reality and act accordingly.

In this sense, I believe that Japan, as the first country to suffer the tragedy of the atomic bomb, must continue to be an advocate for, and raise its voice more emphatically for peace.

Rotblat: Hiroshima and Nagasaki stand as the symbols for why humankind must abolish nuclear weapons. They present an eternal symbol to the world.

Ikeda: The world is surprisingly uninformed about the horrific events of Hiroshima and Nagasaki. As a result, you often hear people declare without hesitation that dropping the atomic bomb helped save many lives or that nuclear weapons help protect the peace. However, the tragic reality is far beyond what any of these people could possibly imagine.

Therefore, I believe it is important for people to understand exactly what occurred at the place where the atomic bomb was dropped. With this in mind, SGI has held the "Nuclear Arms: Threat to Our World" and the "War and Peace" exhibitions at the UN headquarters in New York as well as in Moscow, Beijing, and New Delhi, with the intention of conveying to as many people as possible the horrors and folly of nuclear weapons.

Rotblat: I commend SGI for many years of anti-nuclear and anti-war activities.

Ikeda: I have also persistently urged that all world leaders, especially leaders of the nuclear powers, visit Hiroshima and Nagasaki. I think that nuclear arms reduction talks should be convened in Hiroshima and Nagasaki. Hiroshima and Nagasaki can teach us a lesson about the tragic consequences of those past events. It can also teach us that hope can emerge from such devastation and horror.

Gandhi once said that the power of the human spirit is stronger than nuclear weapons. The way that the people of Hiroshima and Nagasaki have overcome the devastation and suffering of this unprecedented disaster and rebuilt their city will surely inspire hope in the hearts of many. This is also the assertion expressed by my friend, Norman Cousins, the famous American journalist and philosopher.

Rotblat: I knew Norman Cousins, and I believe that he was right. I also believe that Hiroshima and Nagasaki symbolize the utter devastation of nuclear war while simultaneously shining as beacons of hope and optimism for the future. The people of these cities set about rebuilding and returning to their everyday lives, despite the complete destruction and anguish they had experienced. Of course, they could never return to the lives they knew before. Even so, they worked to rebuild their cities and their lives. This is a true demonstration of hope in action.

Ikeda: Professor Rotblat, you participated in the US project for development of nuclear weapons, the Manhattan Project, at first, but you resolutely quit the project. I would like to ask you, where were you on August 6, 1945 when Hiroshima was struck by the atomic bomb. Also, how did you find out about it?

The sad reality of Hiroshima

Rotblat: At that time, I was living in Liverpool, England. I had already left the Manhattan Project and departed from the US. Before I reminisce about that period, I would like to tell you about the course of events that led to my return to England. When I announced my intention to return to England, people in the Defense Agency tried to block my return home by fabricating lies accusing me of wanting to go to England to hand over secrets about the atomic bomb to the USSR.

When it became clear that I could not be prevented from returning to England, I was presented with a condition that I had to agree to before leaving the US. This condition dictated that I must not contact any of my former colleagues who worked at the Los Alamos Laboratory.

Ikeda: By colleagues, you must mean the ones who developed the atomic bomb at the Los Alamos National Laboratory in New Mexico.

Rotblat: Yes. All letters were screened and recorded, so I did not send any letters to my former colleagues. I was afraid that it would put them in danger. As a result, after leaving Los Alamos in December 1944 and returning to Liverpool, I had no idea of what was happening there. This was the context in which I heard the news of the atomic blast. It was August 6, 1945. I heard about it on a BBC news broadcast.

Ikeda: How did you feel when you heard the news?

Rotblat: I was numbed by the shock because, at that time, I still had hope. It was a faint hope, but I had hope that the Americans would be unsuccessful at building the bomb. I thought that since the research had been conducted completely on the basis of theoretical calculations, perhaps at the actual bomb-making stage it might not work. I also harbored hope that even if they were successful at making a bomb, they would not use it, especially against civilian populations.

In other words, even if a bomb were successfully created, it would first of all have to be tested in a remote location such as an uninhabited island. And so I still hoped that the Americans would tell the Japanese, "Look! We have this super weapon," and then the war would be over.

But sadly, reality unfolded quite differently. Man's first atomic bomb was dropped on a civilian population.

Ikeda: The news of the dropping of the atomic bomb was broadcast through the public-address system at Los Alamos. The announcement read, "Just now, one of our explosive devices was successfully detonated in Japan." At that moment, the entire Los Alamos Laboratory erupted in victorious jubilation. However, later that evening a gloomy mood enveloped the celebration party. After the elation and sense of accomplishment wore off, they were left with a sense of regret and foreboding. We are told that this sums up the mood that prevailed at the laboratory.

Setting off a nuclear race: "I am become death"

Rotblat: Personally, I felt a deep sense of despair. It was not simply shock. I was completely overcome with hopelessness. It was an indescribable sense of shock from which it took a long time to recover. This is because I knew that the dropping of the bomb on Hiroshima was just the first step in an extended program of nuclear weapons development.

At that time, I knew that the hydrogen bomb existed, but it was highly classified. I knew about it because my office at Los Alamos was right next to Edward Teller's office. Teller was the scientist who developed the hydrogen bomb, and we spoke frequently. So that is why I knew that a weapon possessing a thousand times more destructive power would be developed next.

At Los Alamos, I had occasion to speak frequently with the prominent physicist Niels Bohr, whom you mentioned previously. He predicted that if the US used the atomic bomb, this would set off a nuclear arms race. He thought that the Soviets would probably manufacture their own bomb, test it somewhere, and want to use it in a war. Then, if nuclear weapons continued to proliferate, this would lead to the annihilation of the human race. This all made me extremely anxious.

Ikeda: Most striking to me was the way that the atomic blast was referred to in religious terms by those who used the nuclear weapons. On August 9, US President Harry Truman prayed, "May God guide us to use it in His ways and for His purposes." Also, after the nuclear test was conducted at Alamogordo, New Mexico, J. Robert Oppenheimer, director of the Los Alamos laboratory, said that he was reminded of a verse from the Hindu epic *Bhagavad-Gita*, "I am become death, destroyer of worlds. …"

My first thought was that these statements reflect a serious understanding of the historical significance of nuclear weapons. But whether consciously or unconsciously, this attitude casts an impenetrable veil of spirituality over nuclear weapons and fails to recognize the users' own responsibility in creating the problem in the first place.

If I were to categorize human history into parts, I would draw the line between the pre-nuclear and post-nuclear periods. This is because, with the introduction of nuclear weapons, for the first time, the extinction of the human race became a conceivable reality. We must never lose sight of the fact, however, that human beings created nuclear weapons.

Rotblat: I became obsessed with the need to discover a way to prevent human extinction. Let me illustrate how driven I was by this goal. When I look back now, I wonder how I ever came up with such a crazy idea. Thinking as a scientist, I looked for a way to halt research in nuclear physics. I wanted to do whatever it took to stop the development of the hydrogen bomb. I thought that this could happen if all the scientists agreed to temporarily halt their research. So I proceeded to contact scientists, primarily physicists at English universities, to convince them that something needed to be done to prevent the extermination of the human race.

The courage to quit

Ikeda: What kind of response did you receive from the scientists?

Rotblat: Many of them did not realize the nature of the problem, and so there was not much reaction. Some of the physicists were sympathetic to my position, but others were completely opposed.

Interestingly, the people who were most opposed were on the left of the political spectrum. They tended to resonate strongly with the communist philosophy. In other words, they argued that if the research on nuclear physics were discontinued, the US would be the only nuclear power possessing the atomic bomb, and that would make it the world's only superpower. It was thought that it would be best to wait until the USSR developed its own atomic bomb before ceasing all research and development. Then, the thinking was that an equal balance of power could be maintained. That is why I gave up. I realized that it would be impossible to halt all research and, realistically speaking, all indications pointed to the inevitable progression of worldwide nuclear research.

Ikeda: Professor Rotblat, I empathize completely with your sense of urgency and concern. In any case, you were moved to action. A person's worth must be determined, not by thoughts, but by actions. Many of the people involved in nuclear weapons research at Los Alamos were very emotionally conflicted about their role. And after the atomic blast, some people were filled with regret. But Professor Rotblat, you were the only one who acted upon your convictions and quit the Manhattan Project before the bomb was dropped.

I know how much courage must have been required to defy the military and political authorities during the war. Soka Gakkai was opposed to Japanese militarism during the Second World War, and Tsunesaburo Makiguchi, our first president died in prison, and our second president, Josei Toda spent two years incarcerated.

2 Mr. Tsunesaburo Makiguchi (right) and Mr. Josei Toda, 1930

Visualizing the impact of nuclear weaponry

Rotblat: Yes, I am familiar with your history. Personally speaking, the atomic bomb did not only fill me with dread, it made me wonder about the survival of the human race. It also made me determined to devote the rest of my life to making sure that nuclear weapons would never again be used.

To begin with, I established the Atomic Scientists' Association in England in order to organize scientists to fight against any effort to use nuclear weapons. This was in 1946. I became the vice-president, and many scientists participated in the organization. Next, I felt impelled to share the reality of nuclear weapons with the public at large, because the average person had no idea about the dangers and threat of nuclear arms.

I poured much of my energy into exhibitions that explained the beneficial uses of nuclear energy as well as its abuse in destructive military campaigns.

Ikeda: They say that sight learning is an effective teaching method that conveys all the necessary information at a glance. From this perspective, the exhibitions are one good way for educating the public. In the days when visual media was less widespread, this was even more true.

SGI has done its best to educate the public and advocate a world without war and the abolition of nuclear weapons through its "Nuclear Arms: Threat to Our World" and the "War and Peace" exhibitions, which have been held in many countries around the globe.

Professor Rotblat, what were the kinds of exhibitions that you were instrumental in planning?

Rotblat: I helped sponsor a mobile exhibition that was carried in a train of two carriages. We called it the Atom Train. The exhibition included a demonstration device that showed the actual detonation mechanism of an atomic bomb. This was our first attempt to convey information and educate the public. This train exhibition traveled through the British Isles and then throughout Europe, and even went as far as the Middle East. We also sold over 53,000 copies of our Atom Train pamphlet.

Ikeda: What an amazing venture! You said that you wanted to devote your energies to benefit humankind, so you switched from the field of nuclear physics to a new path in life. You chose the field of radiation medicine. In England, radiation therapy developed from your achievements. I understand that even now, your discovery of the radioactive element Cobalt-60 is used in the treatment of malignant tumors.

Betrayed by the bomb: turning to medicine

Rotblat: I felt that I was betrayed by the atomic bomb. I consider myself a scientist who strives for the benefit of humankind, not for its destruction. I was motivated to conduct research on the atomic bomb in order to prevent nuclear weapons from being used, since the Nazis were a grave threat. This may be a flawed argument, but this was the reason I participated in this research. Ultimately, however, nuclear weapons came to be used after all.

I felt that if my scientific research was going to be used, I would want to decide how it could be used and to see with my own eyes it being used in beneficial ways. One way that I thought that this could happen was in the field of medicine. Nuclear physics was being used in numerous ways in the field of medicine, so I decided to abandon my ambitions in the field of nuclear physics and specialize in the medical application of physics.

Ikeda: I see. Now I understand exactly how the bombing of Hiroshima impacted on your life so dramatically. You have visited both Hiroshima and Nagasaki. When did you first visit Hiroshima? And what was your purpose at that time?

Rotblat: My first visit to Hiroshima was in 1967. I met with many people, including the mayor of Hiroshima, and also attended a major conference.

At that time, Hiroshima was not completely rebuilt, so here and there you could see the bombed-out remains of buildings. I visited one of these stark skeleton-like buildings, the Atomic Dome. It was a great shock to witness. I had visited Hiroshima for several reasons. One was to see with my own eyes the devastation unleashed upon the city and to help bring about a change in the world in which there would truly be "No more Hiroshimas".

Another reason was related to my area of expertise. As I have mentioned before, I switched my specialty to focus on the medical applications of physics. And at the same time, I began to pursue research on the effect of radiation on the human body, especially over time, and particularly as it related to the development of cancer.

So, accordingly, I visited research institutions and hospitals where atom bomb victims resided. I participated in activities in the US and Japan to support atom bomb victims and conducted research on the effects of radiation. It was extremely important, I felt, to elucidate the impact of radiation.

Visiting Hiroshima and Nagasaki

Ikeda: Did you experience a shift in your perceptions after visiting Hiroshima?

Rotblat: Absolutely. After seeing with my own eyes the devastation wreaked upon Hiroshima, I was able to convey more clearly to others the magnitude of misery inflicted by nuclear weapons.

When I viewed the photographs in the Peace Memorial Museum, I could barely contain my tears. Ever since, I have been urging the museum to establish permanent exhibits in many other places outside Hiroshima. Every town and city should have an atomic bomb exhibit to remind people constantly of the horrors of the atomic bomb. I have traveled the world advocating this idea.

I have also engaged in educational activities. I have spent my later years holding exhibitions, giving lectures and keynote addresses at conferences, and doing all I can to prevent the use of nuclear weapons.

Ikeda: At this point, what lessons do you think humanity should learn from Hiroshima and Nagasaki?

Rotblat: I have a rather broad view of their potential contribution that includes but also goes beyond the effort to abolish nuclear weapons. In other words, I believe that we must strive to create a world without war itself. I have set myself two goals in my life—one short-term and one long-term. My short-term goal is to abolish nuclear weapons, and the long-term goal is to eliminate war entirely. I do not believe that I will live to see either of my objectives achieved within my lifetime, but I believe that ultimately they will be realized.

Our responsibility to past, present and future

Ikeda: Our duty as citizens of the twenty-first century is to work toward a world without war. First of all, we have a responsibility to the past. We live with the knowledge that over one hundred million people have been sacrificed to war in the twentieth century. We have a responsibility to these people. Second, we must consider our responsibility in the present. In today's world, hundreds of millions of people live in abject poverty and are on the verge of starvation. War only aggravates those problems, and moreover, war gives rise to further wars. Humanity must interrupt this vicious circle.

Third, I would like to point out our responsibility to the future. In today's world, wars and the build-up of armaments are not only likely to lead to nuclear war but will surely threaten humanity with their massive power to devastate life systems and the environment on a global scale. If a nuclear war were triggered, humanity's continued existence would be in question.

It is widely thought that the Russell–Einstein Manifesto advocates the abolition of nuclear weapons, but actually it advocates the abolition of war.

Shall we end the human race?

Rotblat: Yes. Even if we are able to eliminate all nuclear weapons, we will still retain the knowledge of how to manufacture them, and it will be impossible to erase that knowledge from humankind's memory. In the future, even if we are able to create a world without nuclear weapons, if a conflict were to erupt between the superpowers, then nuclear weapons would start to be developed and manufactured again within a short period of time, and we would return to the same situation as during the Cold War. Therefore, simply abolishing nuclear weapons is not sufficient.

What concerns me even more, however, is the thought that nuclear weapons will not be the final weapon invented by scientists. With the advance of research, new types of weapons that inflict even greater massive destruction will be developed. Therefore, until humankind learns to coexist without resorting to war, we are not safe. This is the reason that in the Russell–Einstein Manifesto the question was raised, which might seem slightly exaggerated: "Shall we put an end to the human race; or shall mankind renounce war?" This is a reality that we cannot escape.

Ikeda: The current trend, by the way, is to include the use of nuclear weapons in the arsenal of contemporary war tools. I feel very anxious about this trend exemplified by the development of smaller nuclear weapons. The development of nuclear weapons began initially in response to the threat from the Nazis. The reasoning then became "to contain the Soviet Union", and next, it shifted to a deterrent role that held the threat of "massive retaliation" and maintained an understanding of "mutually assured destruction" or MAD.

The ending of the Cold War provided a golden opportunity to end the nuclear age once and for all, but nuclear weapons were retained and now are being considered for use in conventional warfare. In other words, nuclear weapons do not continue to exist out of necessity. Rather, you could say that there are those who need to justify the existence of nuclear weapons by finding a convincing argument.

So, against this illogical backdrop is, as you often say, a persistent "culture of war" in which military might begets even more powerful military force.

Rotblat: Victory will never be achieved by opposing evil with the power of evil. It does not make sense to try to avoid war by using the threat of war. We must learn to resolve our conflicts without resorting to military means. We must not bring human civilization, a miraculous product of millions of years of evolution, to an untimely and tragic end.

Ikeda: When we look at the harsh reality of the international situation, some say that it will be impossible to abolish nuclear weapons. These people, however, are committing the error of predicting the future based on the conditions of our present reality.

As you often mention, during the period before World War II, France and Germany were bitter enemies. Today, however, both countries form the nucleus of the European Union. Examples such as these abound throughout history. A major human weakness is assuming that the reality before our eyes will continue unchanged into the future. We must not forget that the success of the movement to abolish nuclear weapons will be determined by human will.

CHAPTER 3

Living History:
To Survive, to Study when
the World is at War

Ikeda: Professor Rotblat, you were born on November 4, 1908. You are indeed a survivor of the turbulence that swirled around you during the twentieth century. You are an eminent scientist, and the noble trajectory of your life, spent fighting for peace, is a precious guide for the young people of today who must navigate the twenty-first century.

During our discussion, I would like to explore your recollections of your upbringing and the difficult conditions of your young adulthood. I understand that you were born in Warsaw, Poland.

A Polish childhood, a stolen childhood

Rotblat: Yes. When I was born, Warsaw was under the rule of Czarist Russia. At that point, for over one hundred years, Poland had been divided into three parts that were subsumed within the territories of Russia, Germany (Prussia), and Austria.

Ikeda: The first division of Poland by major world powers took place in 1772. Since then, Poland's national boundary has been redrawn many times, causing the Polish people to suffer many continuous hardships and to be labeled "a people without a country". Even so, in spite of over one hundred years of domination by other countries, the people of Poland have never lost their national soul. Their sense of ethnic pride and their culture sustained them through this period. In the arts, for example, Poland has produced many great artists such as Frédéric Chopin (1810–1849) and the poet Adam Mickiewicz (1798–1855).

Rotblat: Although the Polish people experienced such difficult circumstances, my family was relatively affluent, so I remember my early years as a happy time. However, at the age of five, my carefree and untroubled childhood came to a sudden end.

World War I had broken out, and my family was plunged into the worst of circumstances. The family business was dealt a devastating blow by the war. My father was in the transportation business and he had horses and horse-drawn wagons. Most of his customers were in Finland. As soon as the war began, the German army occupied Poland, and business conditions worsened to the point that my father went out of business. Also, the German occupation army confiscated all of my father's horses for the war effort. So my family lost everything, including the means to make a living. And naturally, there was no insurance or means of compensation.

Then after World War I, Poland became independent, but our family was never able to recover from the overwhelming damage that we sustained.

Ikeda: It is tragic that your idyllic childhood was cut short and that your happy family life was destroyed so abruptly.

Rotblat: There were times when my mother would give us two pieces of bread and say, "Here is your food for today." But relatively speaking, those were the good days, because more often, for days at a time, we had nothing to eat. Food was rationed, and we had to wait in line with crowds of people to receive just a little bit of bread. Society was enveloped in rage, disease was rampant, and the children were always hungry. These were the circumstances that had a significant impact on my character development.

We were not only cold and starving, but we were unable to maintain even the most basic sanitation. As a result, I contracted almost every childhood illness there was. And in those days, childhood illnesses were extremely dangerous.

Ikeda: My childhood was also stolen by World War II when society was enveloped in darkness. When I was nine years old, first my eldest brother was drafted, then my other three older brothers were taken one after another. This left me, my younger siblings, and my aging parents. My father suffered from rheumatism. I was entrusted with the care of the family, but it was a big task because I was physically weak and suffered from lung problems.

It was an especially sad and bitter experience for my family to lose my eldest brother, upon whom my parents relied so much. He died on the battlefront in Burma in January 1945, just one day after his birthday. I will never forget my mother's heart-wrenching grief at receiving the news—two years after the end of the war—that my eldest brother had been killed. It was then that a burning rage toward militarism and war was seared into my heart.

Imagination: an alternative world of science fiction

Rotblat: I know exactly what you mean. When I was a child, I knew in my heart that war was the most evil of all human activities. My only enjoyment during those oppressive days was to immerse myself in the fanciful world of science fiction. The sorrow and tragic circumstances of my life caused me all the more to seek an alternative world, a world far removed from my present grim reality, a different world that I could create in my imagination.

I was especially captivated by the works of Jules Verne (1828–1905), who stimulated my interest in science.

Ikeda: His works, *20,000 Leagues Under the Sea* and *Around the World in 80 Days*, are classics that are still loved by Japanese readers today.

Rotblat: That's wonderful. Many of the things that Jules Verne imagined actually became reality many years later, for example, television or putting a man on the moon. At that time, however, his ideas were relegated to the world of pure fantasy.

Ikeda: It's well known that Konstantin Tsiolkovsky (1857–1935), the father of Russian space travel, was deeply influenced by Jules Verne's science-fiction accounts of travel to the moon. So the dreams that we develop in childhood have a lasting impact on our lives.

When I was younger, I was involved in compiling a children's magazine and served as the editor-in-chief. The war had just ended, and people were in a general state of confusion and distress. I poured all my energy into this endeavor, because I wanted to give children, whose everyday lives were so grim, a chance to have big hopes and dreams. I wanted to nurture in them the strength to go on living. I solicited writing from the best authors of the day, and featured some of the world's great works, including biographies, as well as science-fiction novels and other science-related stories. I also included plenty of illustrations depicting joyful and happy situations.

Rotblat: This is the first time I have heard about your efforts to publish an inspiring magazine for children and youth.

Ikeda: I have a lot of precious memories of those days. Partly because I was in poor health then, I was an avid reader as well.

During the war, I was not able to read as much as I would have liked, but when I worked at a military manufacturing plant, I would read during my lunch hour on the lawn in the middle of the factory courtyard. This was one of my precious few enjoyments. Today, children are bombarded with a plethora of amusements, and the decline in reading is decried. But during my childhood, there was little else but books, so perhaps we were able to appreciate the attraction of books and the valuable world they could provide us.

Eyes opened to possibilities of science

Rotblat: That's true. In my case, reading books as a youth helped open my eyes to the possibilities of science. I told myself, "If science has such power and promise, why are these science-fiction stories merely fiction? I'm sure that the power of science can be harnessed for the good of humanity and the world."

This is when I began to view science as not only a discipline for discovering truth, but also as a means to save humankind. I was hopeful that science could be used to create a world in which war was unnecessary, people's hardships would be alleviated, and happiness would be universal. Ultimately, the reason I decided to become a scientist was to benefit humanity.

Ikeda: I feel that I have a sense of the source of your unwavering commitment, as a scientist, to peace and humanism.

Rotblat: It was not easy to become a scientist. First of all, the requirements for enrolling in the university were graduation from high school and passing the university entrance examination. Unfortunately for me, my family did not have the funds to pay for my high-school tuition. From a very young age, I had to be responsible for earning my own living expenses. I was financially independent at the age of fifteen and was determined that if I could not go to high school, I would still study on my own. That was when I began working as a manual laborer doing electrical work, and at night I would study physics.

Ikeda: You must have had a very difficult time as a young man, but now you have become a world-renowned nuclear physicist. I think that your inspiring story will surely give hope and courage to many young people.

In my case, after the war, my family did not have the wherewithal to send me to regular day school either, so I went to night school to get an education while working by day. You could call it a school, but this was post-war Tokyo, so it was a shell of a building that amazingly was still standing. Cold wind blew in through the broken windows in winter, and in the classrooms, bare lightbulbs swayed in the breeze. Even so, I would not have traded anything in the world for the joy I felt at being able to study.

While I was going to night school, I happened to meet a marvelous educator. This turned out to be the single most important experience of my life. He encouraged me, saying, "Adversity builds character. People must live their ideals and not lose hope."

As I heard you speak, I was reminded of what I learned during my night-school courses.

Rotblat: Eventually, I was able to attend the Free University of Poland in Warsaw. This university was expressly for working people, and so the classes were held in the evening. At the university, I met Dr. Ludwik Wertenstein. He was the head of the physics department and was a student of Madame Curie.

A teacher to believe in

Ikeda: Professor Rotblat, did you ever have the opportunity to meet Madame Curie?

Rotblat: Yes. It was some time later, but I met her just once, just before she died. During my student days, I was also very fortunate to encounter Dr. Wertenstein. There were hardly any radiologists or physicists in Poland at that time. Dr. Wertenstein was the director of the Radiological Laboratory of Warsaw and was conducting research on radioactivity. At that time, he was one of only a handful of people in this field in the world.

Dr. Wertenstein was not only a first-rate scientist, he was also a very fine person who deserves recognition as a dedicated humanist. I owe a large debt of gratitude to Dr. Wertenstein, who taught me about physics and nuclear physics as well as the fundamental approach to scientific inquiry. Furthermore, he also taught me about the importance of holding ethical values as a scientist. I was truly blessed to have a teacher whom I could respect as a researcher, educator, and, above all, as a person.

Ikeda: There is no happier event in life than meeting a great mentor. I met my lifelong mentor, Josei Toda, right after the war when I was nineteen years of age. I think this was the age at which you met your teacher, Dr. Wertenstein. During the war, Mr. Toda suffered persecution and was held in prison. This fact was extremely significant for me. This was because I lost all faith in those irresponsible adults and intellectuals who, while following the military authorities during the war, suddenly changed their attitude when the war ended, and became critical of militarism and began advocating peace. I thought that I could trust Mr. Toda because here was a person who had held on to his own beliefs and was put into prison for doing so. I felt a powerful attraction to Mr. Toda's personality from the moment I met him.

Later, I established the Toda Institute of Global Peace and Policy Research. It was a great privilege that we were able to confer the first Toda Prize for Peace Research on you, Professor Rotblat. Mr. Toda was born in the year 1900, so he is of the same generation as you. Because of that fact, I was filled with even deeper emotion on that occasion

Rotblat: Likewise, I felt greatly honored to receive the prize. Mr. Toda was a heroic peace advocate and a martyr for peace. I regret that I could not meet him.

Ikeda: The Toda Institute, whose underlying theme is dialogue among civilizations, has carried on Mr. Toda's passionate desire for peace by promoting research projects related to the abolition of nuclear weapons and to building world peace.

Rotblat: In a short span of time, the Toda Institute has established itself as an important force in tackling the enormous work of education, research, and publishing activities. I hold the Toda Institute's accomplishments in high regard.

Dr. Wertenstein provided constant support. I received my degree in 1932, and afterwards he helped me to obtain work in the research institute.

The salary was a pittance, but at least I was able to begin conducting scientific research. This launched my journey in the field of science, a journey that I am still pursuing.

Ikeda: In 1939, you traveled to England and began research at the University of Liverpool.

Rotblat: It was Dr. Wertenstein who arranged for me to study abroad. In 1934, I had discovered a new radioactive element called Cobalt-60. As a result, my name became more known in scientific circles. This resulted in invitations to work at two research laboratories.

One came from the Frederic Joliet-Curie Research Institute in Paris, France. As you know, Joliet is the husband of Madame Curie's daughter, Irene. Later, this husband-and-wife team received the Nobel Peace Prize for their discovery of artificial radioactivity, and their research institute in Paris became an important center for scientists.

Ikeda: Speaking of Madame Curie, in the gardens of the Soka Women's College, which I founded, there is a statue of Madame Curie holding a flask.

Seven years ago [1998] during her visit to Japan, Ellen, the granddaughter of Madame Curie, visited our campus and spent some time chatting with our students. The students were thrilled to be able to meet her.

Rotblat: That's very nice. That must have been a very meaningful experience for the students.

The other invitation I had was from Professor James Chadwick of the University of Liverpool. At that time, Professor Chadwick was well known for discovering the neutron.

Love and loss: a woman named Tola

Ikeda: So you were torn between choosing England or France for the site of your research?

Rotblat: To tell the truth, I had many sleepless nights. I was confident of my French-language skills to a certain point, and Paris held a certain attraction, but in the end, I decided to go to Liverpool.

Another factor that affected my decision was that Professor Chadwick was building a cyclotron, a kind of ion accelerator that is used to artificially bombard atomic nuclei. I had in mind that I would like to build one in Poland, too, so I decided to study under Professor Chadwick. The only problem was that I could read English, but I was a novice at English conversation. And worse yet, the language spoken in Liverpool was not ordinary English. It was a language unto itself, and it left me totally bewildered.

When I first came to England, I received an annual grant award of £120. The scholarship was just enough for one person to get by on, living very frugally, and the amount of money that could be sent from Poland was strictly limited. This was not enough to support two people; consequently, my wife, Tola, had to stay behind in Poland.

Ikeda: Your life as a researcher at that time in England must have been difficult. Was there ever a time when you wanted to discontinue your research and return to Poland?

Rotblat: I never got to the point that I wanted to return to Poland, but I did consider moving to Paris to work at another research institute. I actually wrote a letter to Tola telling her that I was thinking of changing course and transferring to the Paris institute. She wrote back saying, "If you do that, you'll regret it your entire life. So, do your best to see it through to the end."

So, I heeded my wife's advice and dedicated myself to my work. And in the first several months, I was able to do some meaningful research. This in turn led to a renewal of my scholarship for the following year. The research grant was again £120. This was an extremely coveted award, and I was the first foreigner who had received it.

Ikeda: Your wife must have been overjoyed.

Rotblat: When I learned that I would be receiving the scholarship, I immediately determined that I would bring my wife to England. So, at one point, I returned to Warsaw in August of 1939. But just before we were to leave for England, she came down with severe appendicitis. She had to have surgery immediately, and the doctor forbade her to make the long, difficult journey by train to England. In those days, only the very rich could afford the luxury of flying. I had to return to Liverpool, so I went ahead, and my wife was to join me there later.

Ikeda: The two of you were then separated by fate.

Rotblat: Yes. I arrived in Liverpool on August 30. Two days later, on September 1, Nazi Germany led by Hitler invaded Poland.

Ikeda: And this marked the beginning of World War II.

Rotblat: Several months passed before I had any communication with my wife. Thanks to the International Committee of the Red Cross, we were able to correspond by mail. As soon as we were able to correspond, I immediately renewed my efforts to bring her to England. Mr. Arnold McNair, the vice-chancellor of the University of Liverpool, sympathized with our situation. He suggested that my wife go to a neutral country, where she could be given an English passport. Also, on the advice of Professor Chadwick, I wrote a letter to Professor Niels Bohr who was in Copenhagen, Denmark.

Ikeda: At that time, Professor Bohr was being targeted by the Nazis, and even though his scientist friends and acquaintances tried to persuade him to flee to a safe place, he stayed in Copenhagen and was able to save many people.

Rotblat: Professor Bohr was a great man. He was kind and considerate. He notified me that he had begun processing a transit visa for Tola. Unfortunately, however, soon after, Denmark was also invaded by the Nazis.

I implemented a second strategy at the same time as the first. I tried to have the passport processed in Belgium and asked for help from my cousin who lived in Brussels. But the Belgian processing took an extremely long period of time, and so by the time the process was almost complete, the Germans had attacked Belgium.

Ikeda: In no time, the Nazi rampage swept throughout Europe.

Rotblat: That's right. The third strategy I tried was to go through Italy. Here I called upon the Toeplitzs, an influential family that lived in Milan. They were relatives of Dr. Wertenstein. Italy was part of the Tripartite Pact (the Rome–Berlin–Tokyo Axis), but Italy had not yet formally declared war. Tola was to go from Poland to Italy by train through Czechoslovakia and Austria. If she could have got that far, she would have been able to reach England. The Toeplitzs were able to secure a visa for her. All the preparations had been made, and in June 1940, I received a message informing me that Tola had actually boarded the train bound for the Italian border.

Ikeda: By this time, nearly a year had passed since you had returned to Poland to bring your wife back to England. It must have been a very, very long year for you.

Rotblat: Unfortunately, I received the news about my wife's journey at the same time that we learned that Mussolini had declared war on England. For a time after that, I clung to the hope that, since my wife already had a visa, she would somehow be able to reach Italy, and then it would be easier for her to leave Italy than Poland.

I waited for what seemed like an eternity. Then, a long time later, I received a letter. It was sent from Warsaw. My wife had been prevented from crossing the border, so she had never been able to leave Poland. Again at the end of 1940, I received another letter from my wife. After that, only silence.

Ikeda: What a heart-rending story. You have not discussed these personal details of your past publicly before. You must have kept this buried deep in your heart. I can only imagine the depth of your regret and sorrow. As a Buddhist, I pray for your wife's peaceful repose.

Rotblat: This has been the saddest experience of my entire life. Stalin once said, "A single death is a tragedy, a million deaths is a statistic." Based on this perspective, my wife Tola's death is a statistical fact. Her death had become a statistic. She was one of six million who perished in Poland during World War II.

Ironically, around that time, I busied myself in the design of weaponry that could increase that death rate many times.

Ikeda: Professor Rotblat, you have fought for peace on behalf of yourself as well as your wife. I am sure that all this time, she has always been with you in your heart, inspiring you and encouraging you.

In the introduction that you kindly wrote to a volume of my poetry, your outrage against war and passion for peace are clearly expressed. You write,

> At any given moment in history, precious few voices are heard crying out for justice. But, now more than ever, those voices must rise above the din of vio-

lence and hatred. … If the new century is to be one of peace, if we are to leave behind the fear and tragedy that has so scarred the world's landscape, then we must focus once more on the preciousness of human beings and of life.[1]

As we approach the sixtieth year after the war, we recall its wretched and cruel lessons and realize that we must put a stop to this tragic circle of war and violence. I am heartened and honored to join you among those voices emphatically calling for justice to usher in a new era of peace and harmony among all the peoples of the world.

CHAPTER 4

The Conscience of a Nuclear Physicist: Quitting the Manhattan Project

Ikeda: During World War II many scientists participated in the Manhattan Project to develop nuclear weapons in the US, but Professor Rotblat, you were the only one who felt that the Germans would not be able to build an atomic bomb, and so you quit the project of your own accord halfway through.

Rotblat: Participating in research activities in the Manhattan Project was very traumatic. Some of the participants continued to feel the after-effects of their experience throughout their entire lives, and I would count myself among those.

I first earned my degree in the field of nuclear physics, as you mentioned, in 1932. That year is significant in the history of science because important discoveries were made in rapid succession. James Chadwick, who later invited me to study in England, discovered the neutron; Harold Clayton Urey discovered heavy hydrogen; and Ernest Lawrence invented the cyclotron. All three of these scientists participated in the Manhattan Project.

Personally speaking: the dawn of nuclear physics

Ikeda: So, indeed, you truly began your research activity with the dawn of nuclear physics.

Rotblat: That's right. As I mentioned in our previous discussion, after I received my degree, I began my research at the Radiological Laboratory of

Warsaw under Dr. Ludwik Wertenstein. Then, several years later in 1939, nuclear physics came to a major turning point.

The pivotal event was the discovery of fission, that is, splitting the atom. Just as the nucleus of a plant divides, it was confirmed that the nucleus of one atom would divide into two small atomic nuclei. This phenomenon was unexpected by most scientists. The greatest significance of this discovery for humankind lay in the tremendous energy created by splitting the atom.

Ikeda: You also heard about the news very soon.

Rotblat: I first heard about the news of splitting of the atom in January 1939. Immediately thereafter, the Germans Lise Meitner and Otto Frisch published their study in a scientific journal. After hearing the news of the discovery, I confirmed this by conducting an experiment in which I found that by bombarding atomic nuclei with neutrons, the atoms split, and concurrently, a number of neutrons were released.

Then when the released neutrons clashed with other atomic nuclei in their vicinity, again further splitting occurred and numerous neutrons were released. Energy is extracted from this process by slowing down and managing this chain reaction, and this is the mechanism by which a nuclear reactor works. I predicted, however, that if this chain reaction occurred within a short period of time, the splitting atoms would create a massive amount of energy that would have a monumental explosive power.

Ikeda: In other words, Professor Rotblat, are you saying that you predicted that the phenomenon of splitting the atom would be applied to the manufacture of weaponry?

Rotblat: Yes, but as soon as I had this thought, I tried to vanquish it from my mind. I would imagine that this is similar to the behavior of an incurably ill person stubbornly refusing to acknowledge the first symptoms of an illness.

I continued to be upset by the magnitude of the threat. I felt certain that someone would take this idea and try to implement it. It was not even in my wildest imaginings that I would myself try to execute this idea. After all, I was brought up on humanitarian principles, and I had always felt that science must be put to use in service to humankind. The very thought that I would use my knowledge to further the creation of such a dreadful weapon was abhorrent in the extreme.

Ikeda: Did you ever share this thought with other persons or ask their opinions about it then?

Rotblat: No. For a while I did not speak to anyone about it. Shortly thereafter, my plans to go to England were decided, and I was so busy every day that the menace of an atomic bomb receded somewhat from my mind. But I was still concerned about what would happen if the Nazis developed the bomb. Judging from Hitler's blatant declaration of world domination, if the Nazis were able to develop the atomic bomb, I was convinced that they would use it.

Shortly after I went to England, an article touching on the application of atomic power to military weaponry was published in a German journal. It appeared in June. After that, my unease and distress grew more and more intense.

Ikeda: Of course. So, you felt that there was an increasing possibility that the Germans would develop the atomic bomb.

Rotblat: Yes. As I mentioned in our previous conversation, I returned to Poland for a brief visit in 1939. During my stay, I visited Dr. Wertenstein and confided in him. I showed him the rough calculations and discussed with him my thoughts about the menace of nuclear weapons. He seemed not to have considered the idea before, but he said that what I described was theoretically possible. When I asked him if the manufacture of nuclear weapons should be allowed, he said, "Personally speaking, I would not participate in that kind of endeavor." Dr. Wertenstein was the kind of person who lived by his convictions, no matter what the circumstances.

I had hoped that Dr. Wertenstein would help me figure out how to deal with this whole matter, but he told me that, ultimately, I was the only one who could make decisions for myself. So, I resolved to let my conscience be my guide.

Connections: weaponry and the power of the atom

Ikeda: During this same period, a number of nuclear physicists around the world began to make similar connections between discoveries in nuclear physics and the development of weaponry based on the power of the atom. Leo Szilárd, the Hungarian-born physicist who drafted the famous Einstein letter urging the US government to begin an atomic research program, and others were actively engaged in countering the German threat. Szilárd participated in the Manhattan Project, but he was opposed to dropping the atomic bomb on Hiroshima. After the war, you as well as Szilárd were active as members of the Pugwash Conferences.

Rotblat: The event that helped me make a definitive decision on my participation in developing the atomic bomb was Germany's invasion of Poland. I was appalled at the massive military might used by Hitler's army and the panic it spread among the people. I felt that our only option was to prevent the Germans from using the atomic bomb by having one of our own and threatening retaliation, if necessary. But I never imagined that we would actually use an atomic bomb on the Nazis or anyone else.

Ikeda: You are describing the previously mentioned "nuclear deterrence" theory, aren't you?

Rotblat: That's right. However, in retrospect, I recognize the foolishness of this idea, because threats would have had no impact on a psychopath such as Hitler. If he had possessed a nuclear weapon, he probably would have used it even though he would have known that he would be inviting massive retaliation.

   At that time, there were hardly any leading physicists remaining at the University of Liverpool, because most of them had been recruited to work on developing the nascent radar technology. Radar was considered to be the most critical technology for waging modern warfare. One of its first accomplishments was the major role it played in preventing the Germans from invading England.

Ikeda: Your story gives a sense of the highly charged atmosphere of those times.

Rotblat: In late October of 1939, I presented a research plan to Professor Chadwick to help develop the potential of the nuclear bomb. Chadwick did not give me a clear response to my proposal. I learned later that around that time other English scientists had had the same idea and were trying to initiate the same kind of research. Apparently, at the University of Birmingham, Otto Frisch, whom I mentioned before, and exiled scientist Rudolf Peierls were already beginning to conduct research. Chadwick maintained strict confidentiality, so I only learned of this research activity much later. Several days after speaking with Professor Chadwick, he gave me permission to go ahead with the research and assigned me two young assistants. So, I was able to begin my research at the end of 1939.

Manhattan, MAUD and projects to develop a nuclear bomb

Ikeda: Then, this means that you began your nuclear development research in 1939, earlier than the Manhattan Project, which was begun in the US.

Rotblat: Yes. In the US at that time, it was thought that an atomic bomb could not be manufactured due to unresolved technical difficulties. And anyway, the emphasis was on research to harness the power of atomic energy, with a focus on atomic reactor research, rather than on making an atomic bomb. The University of Chicago spearheaded this research.

So, it is fair to say that research on realizing the potential of an atomic bomb was first begun in England.

Ikeda: Yes. Enrico Fermi and his colleagues at the University of Chicago were doing experiments with a small nuclear reactor that they had built in the underground squash courts of the university. In December 1942, they succeeded in creating the world's first self-sustaining nuclear chain reaction. As you described, in the beginning, the US research was oriented to the use of nuclear energy, but eventually it became linked to the development of an atomic bomb.

Rotblat: Yes. Enrico Fermi participated in the Manhattan Project, too.

Ikeda: Speaking of the University of Chicago, I visited the campus about thirty years ago, in January 1975. I was struck by a monument commemorating the development of nuclear energy that was quietly tucked away in a corner of the campus. Coincidentally, one week prior to my visit, I had visited the UN Headquarters in New York and handed the UN secretary-general a ten-million-signature petition demanding the abolition of nuclear weapons.

In any case, you were conducting research in England, and before long, you proceeded to the US, where you participated in the Manhattan Project. Please tell what led you to participate in the Manhattan Project.

Rotblat: In those days, I worked closely with Otto Frisch and other people at the University of Birmingham in England. In 1941, we were able to prove theoretically the potential for a nuclear bomb. The English project was code-named MAUD (or the MAUD Committee). The English scientists had to contend with wartime conditions, which included daily German air raids and the lack of major funding and equipment necessary for this kind of development project.

It was under these circumstances that Mark Oliphant, a University of Birmingham physicist, leaked word of the MAUD project during a trip to the US. This and several other factors combined to provide the impetus for the US to initiate a formal project to manufacture an atomic bomb. Robert Oppenheimer was appointed as the director of the project, which came to be called the Manhattan Project. The project was conducted in Los Alamos in northern New Mexico where a research laboratory was built.

Then, in August 1943, US President Franklin D. Roosevelt and English Prime Minister Winston Churchill met in Quebec, Canada and reached an agreement in which English researchers would participate in the Manhattan Project. Professor Chadwick was selected as the head of the group representing the English researchers.

Ikeda: I see. So, you were designated by Professor Chadwick to participate in the Manhattan Project.

Rotblat: That's right. Professor Chadwick and the others left for the US at the end of 1943, but I departed about a month later, in January 1944. Before we left for the US, however, we had no idea where we were going. All we were told was that we would be going to a destination called "Y". Only after we arrived in Washington were we told that "Y" stood for the Los Alamos laboratory in New Mexico.

Ikeda: And now, the Los Alamos National Laboratory plays a significant role in the nuclear weapons industry. How would you describe the place in those days?

Rotblat: We were not allowed to tell anyone in England of our whereabouts. If ever we wanted to write to someone, our letter would be sent to Washington to a representative of the English research group, then it would be mailed from there. For domestic correspondence, our return address had to be a post office box, No.1663, in Santa Fe, New Mexico. All letters were subject to censorship, so we had to submit outgoing correspondence unsealed to the post office for inspection.

Strictly speaking, this kind of censorship is illegal. Among the scientists there were some who attempted to outwit the censorship. Dick Feynman, a young man at the time who later received the Nobel Prize, was particularly accomplished at getting around the rules.

Political weapon: a breach of faith

Ikeda: This is the first time I've heard of this kind of thing. It must have been especially challenging to work in that kind of environment. Prominent scientists from around the world who had received the Nobel Prize or those who later received it were included in the Manhattan Project. It makes me shudder to think that the most brilliant minds in the world gathered together to develop a weapon that could annihilate the human race. This makes me realize the insanity of war all the more.

Rotblat: A decisive moment for me came in March of 1944. At the time I was living in Professor Chadwick's house, and occasionally General Leslie Groves, who was in charge of the Manhattan Project, would come to visit the Chadwicks. In our conversations, he would share some of the gossip going around in the military circles. Once, he told us that the real objective of building the bomb was, of course, to subdue the Soviet Union. These may not have been his exact words, but they reflect what he meant to say.

I felt a keen sense of betrayal at hearing his words, a sense that the US had committed a breach of faith against its allies. He spoke at a time when thousands of Soviet soldiers were dying every day on the eastern front in order to defeat the German army and to buy time for the Allied Powers to prepare for a landing on the European continent.

Ikeda: This is important historical evidence. So, you discovered in the general's words the true intent of the US leadership's plans for using the nuclear bomb.

Rotblat: Yes. Up until that point, I had felt compelled to conduct my research in order to prevent the Nazis from being victorious. But now I understood that the weapon which we were developing was being created for a different purpose. It was to be used as a strategic political weapon against people who were making the ultimate sacrifice on our behalf. I am not saying that all Americans thought we should develop the nuclear bomb to gain advantage over the Soviets. However, among the military leadership, there must have been many who advocated this approach.

After I heard General Groves' revelation, I began to feel that I was at Los Alamos for the wrong reason. I felt as if the soil beneath my feet was beginning to crumble. Moreover, in mid-1944, the war situation had changed, and the German army had begun gradually to retreat.

Ikeda: A major development in the war in 1944 was that in January, the Soviet troops were able to break the over 900-day siege of Leningrad. Then, in May, German troops retreated from the Crimean Peninsula. Also, on June 6, Operation Overlord, part of the Normandy campaign, was launched, and within approximately ninety days, the Allied Powers were able to win back all of France from the Nazis. On the Pacific front, in 1944, the Japanese had failed in their Imphal campaign. In July, Japanese forces had been completely annihilated in Saipan. Signs of Japanese defeat were becoming clearer.

Plausible lies and political pressure

Rotblat: I began to feel that it was inconceivable that the Germans would be successful in developing the nuclear bomb when even we in the US were having difficulties. Then, in October, the clincher came when Professor Chadwick learned the latest news from the intelligence agency that confirmed that the Germans had discontinued their nuclear bomb program.

I realized then that there was absolutely no reason for me to be at the Los Alamos National Laboratory. I immediately submitted a request to return to England.

Ikeda: It sounds as if it was a simple matter, but actually, it was a very courageous decision. Your quitting the Manhattan Project made the authorities suspicious of you and put your entire future in jeopardy. After all, you were someone who was privy to top-secret government information. I have heard that numerous obstacles were put in your path.

Rotblat: That was certainly the case. The project was under the jurisdiction of the military, and so admitting me, against my will, to a mental hospital would have been a distinct possibility.

I submitted my request for dismissal from the project, and after a while, I received a very troubling response from Professor Chadwick. He said that when he conveyed my request to the intelligence officer at Los Alamos, the officer showed him a dossier that he claimed showed conclusive evidence that would convict me and lead to a severe sentence. In other words, he thought I was a spy. According to the dossier, I had already made arrangements with contacts in Santa Fe to return to England, and my plan was to parachute into Soviet-controlled Poland and divulge nuclear bomb secrets to the Soviets.

It is a fact that I conversed with people in Santa Fe, but the claim of an alleged "plan" was totally baseless. When I pointed out each error in the report created by the intelligence officers, it was clear that they had fabricated the entire story.

Ikeda: Baseless rumors are like that. They sound convincing, are intentionally spread, and are designed to smear honest people. Such false rumors must be clearly exposed and put down. In situations like this, you must raise your voice and speak the truth courageously, questioning the foundation and supporting evidence of the rumors by seeking the facts of "when", "where", and "who". Otherwise, the story takes on a life of its own.

Rotblat: When the scheme was revealed, it completely embarrassed the director of the intelligence agency, and he had to admit that the dossier was a sham. Even so, he made me promise not to talk to anyone regarding the real reason that I wanted to leave the Manhattan Project. He was afraid that my story would create turmoil, and that this would reverberate among the other scientists. I consulted with Professor Chadwick, and we agreed to let people know that I was leaving for personal reasons, that I was concerned about my wife in Poland.

Ikeda: Actually, at that time, isn't it true that you did not know your wife's whereabouts, and you had not received any correspondence from her?

The records of a life: lost, confiscated, destroyed

Rotblat: Yes, that's right. In any case, I began my journey to England on Christmas Eve of 1944. But then, another crisis arose. Before I left Los Alamos, I had packed all my belongings in a sturdy storage trunk. When I had come to the US from England I had assumed that, after I had completed my responsibilities, I would return immediately to Poland. So I carried all my belongings with me.

When I was at Los Alamos, I bought a lot of books. Most of them were about physics, because I thought that they would be useful in Poland after the war. I also had notes from my unclassified experiments, letters, photographs, and a ship's logbook. In other words, this was a record of my entire life. The belongings I had left in Poland had been destroyed during the war, and so the materials in this box represented the belongings that were indispensable to me.

Before leaving the US, I stopped for a few days at Professor Chadwick's house in Washington. When I left his place, Professor Chadwick helped me put my trunk on the train to New York. But a few hours later when I arrived in New York, the trunk was missing. And even though I searched everywhere, I was not able to find it.

Ikeda: It is hard to imagine that this was a simple theft and not a calculated confiscation of your belongings. Even after the war, you faced many difficulties and were treated like a spy, labeled as a security risk, and even refused entry into the US. You always followed your conscience, however, and declared your opposition to the development of nuclear weapons. Your example is a beacon of hope and conscience in the history of science.

During the same period, in Japan, my teacher Josei Toda, our second president, and Tsunesaburo Makiguchi, Soka Gakkai's first president, both opposed Japanese militarism and were incarcerated for their beliefs. Makiguchi died in prison. The two men were imprisoned on July 6, 1943, just before Churchill and Roosevelt met for their Quebec conference. In November 1944, you quit the Manhattan Project, and in the same month, Makiguchi passed away in prison.

Josei Toda, who survived his mentor, was released from prison and devoted himself to expanding the peaceful power of the people. His legacy to us, who were young at the time, was his Declaration Against Nuclear Weapons. His declaration serves as the source of inspiration for Soka Gakkai's peace and nuclear abolition movement.

Incidentally, were there other scientists involved with the Manhattan Project who felt as you did?

Pure research and social applications: who decides?

Rotblat: This has been a major issue for me. Clearly, most of the scientists did not expect General Groves to terminate the project even if the Germans surrendered. Yet, just as I did, many of them had agreed to participate in the project because they wanted to stop the Nazi threat. But why did they continue their research even after the Nazi threat had been removed?

The justification offered most often was that they pursued their research for the sake of inquiry into pure, basic science. In other words, they were intensely eager to actually prove the theoretical calculations and predictions they had made. It was the feeling of these scientists that society should enter into a discussion about the use of nuclear bombs only after the nuclear experiments.

Ikeda: Simply speaking, because of their scientific curiosity, they wanted to see with their own eyes what they could produce.

In Japan, following the bombing of Hiroshima and Nagasaki, a rumor circulated that claimed that Kyoto was to be the third target. When a certain Japanese physicist heard this, he exclaimed, "This is a golden opportunity for physicists. I'm going to the summit of Mount Hiei to carefully observe the blast." And so he actually climbed to the highest peak of Mount Hiei and set up his measurement instruments.

This anecdote cannot be explained away as the insane raving of one crazy scientist. In a sense, it articulates a theme in the discussion of science and civilization, an issue that I would like to revisit.

Rotblat: Other scientists put off dealing with the problem by believing that the atomic bomb would bring the war with Japan to a swift end and thereby save many American lives. These scientists intended to put their energies into activities to make sure that this bomb would never be used again after peace was restored.

The claim that the bomb helped end the war with Japan more quickly has many questionable aspects. For one, the Japanese leaders were already exploring ways to end the war. Furthermore, many other people who felt that the nuclear bomb project should be halted when the German threat faded away did not clearly make their views known, because they were concerned that saying so would ruin their careers.

Ikeda: I see. I can understand the complexity of the situation. At the same time, I am deeply impressed by your courageous decision, as a scientist, to follow your social conscience.

Rotblat: Only a minority of scientists among my colleagues thought that the project should be terminated because the German threat had dissipated. The majority of scientists did not feel any pangs of conscience. They were content to leave completely to others the question of how their research was to be used.

Today, in many countries we see a very similar situation with regard to research related to military projects. However, the issue that most worries me and leaves me at a loss is the absence of ethical conduct under wartime conditions. The problem is that once a war begins, our moral consciousness is cast aside. I myself saw this happen many times. Therefore, it is most important to prevent hostile conditions from arising in the first place.

Ikeda: This is a very crucial point to consider in the discussion of war and peace in today's world. Once the wheels of war start to turn, they run out of control and crush many lives in their path. When confronted with the brutality of war, calm judgment and rational thinking don't stand a chance. That is why I agree with you, Professor Rotblat, that war itself must be opposed absolutely. Yet, modern civilization continues to proceed undeterred though fraught with the danger of war.

By possessing weapons of mass destruction capable of slaughtering all of humankind ten times over, we court the danger of making a mistake that cannot be revoked. Though seemingly circuitous, opening up channels for dialogue is by far the most realistic and common sense approach to building peace.

CHAPTER 5

The Power of a Name:
The Russell–Einstein Manifesto

Ikeda: The year 2005 marks the fiftieth anniversary of the Russell–Einstein Manifesto to which you are a signatory, and the sixtieth anniversary of the dropping of the atomic bomb on Hiroshima and Nagasaki. I believe that we should make these significant occasions major pivotal events designed to carry out our responsibility to humanity.

Rotblat: The Russell–Einstein Manifesto was an urgent call to scientists to participate in conferences to discuss ways to avoid the imminent danger of nuclear war. At the same time, it sought to focus the public's attention on every person's duty to work for the survival and continuation of the human race.

Considering that war is itself a threat to humanity, war is what really should be abolished. The Manifesto ends with the following solemn warning. "We appeal as human beings to human beings: Remember your humanity, and forget the rest. If you can do so, the way lies open to a new Paradise; if you cannot, there lies before you the risk of universal death."

Must human existence rely on military might?

Ikeda: That is perhaps the most famous passage in the Manifesto. To forge a path to a world without war, it is essential that we analyze the structure of alliances between the military, industrial, and academic spheres and also reevaluate the assumption that human existence must rely on military might.

The reason for considering these issues is that in order to contest the political, economic, and scientific premises that argue for the necessity of military might, it is important to point out the reckless and harmful aspects—in other words, we must bring to bear the perspective of humanism.

The Russell–Einstein Manifesto derives its greatness from this corner-stone of humanism. Two years after the Manifesto was made public, my mentor Josei Toda announced his Declaration Against Nuclear Weapons. In his denunciation of nuclear weapons, he also expressed the humanistic insights that informed his perspective. He understood nuclear weapons to be a product of man's murderous instinct and absolute evil.

Rotblat: Two approaches to nuclear weapons have been taken. One is the legal approach, and the second is the moral approach. Mr. Toda, as a religious person, took the latter. I believe that he was right to do so.

Ikeda: I am sure he would have been honored by your acknowledgment of his efforts. On the fiftieth anniversary of the Russell–Einstein Manifesto, I would like very much to ask about the process that led to its achivement.

The Manifesto was announced on July 9, 1955. In January of the previous year, the US announced its policy of "Massive Retaliation", and in

3. The Russell–Einstein Manifesto is announced, 1955.

March tested a hydrogen bomb on Bikini Atoll that was 1000 times more destructive than the bomb dropped on Hiroshima. In 1953, the Soviet Union had already tested a hydrogen bomb, and in February of 1955, the British would commence manufacture of their own hydrogen bomb. In May of that same year, in response to the founding of NATO, the Soviets formed the Warsaw Pact. The Manifesto was announced in the midst of this tension surrounding the proliferation of nuclear weapons.

Rotblat: Around the time of the birth of the Manifesto, I had been in conversations with Bertrand Russell. I had told him about the catastrophic consequences of nuclear war, and he discussed this in his 1954 Christmas broadcast. He wanted ordinary citizens all over the world to be aware of how frightening the effects of nuclear war would be on the entire world, particularly with the advent of thermo-nuclear weapons.

Public response to "Man's Peril"

Ikeda: I believe you are referring to Bertrand Russell's document entitled "Man's Peril". I have heard that this became the foundation for the Russell–Einstein Manifesto, which came later.

Rotblat: That is correct. The broadcast drew a considerable public response—the primary one being, in this critical situation, the desire on the part of the public for scientists to unite and find a way to prevent nuclear war.

Russell felt the need to inform politicians, scientists, and the general public about the dangers of nuclear arms. He thought that if Nobel Laureates, including the world's most prominent scientists, officially lent their voices to the cry to abolish nuclear weapons, then this would have a major impact. At that time—and indeed throughout the history of science—the most preeminent scientist in the world was Albert Einstein, and so Russell determined to ask him to be a signatory. He sent him a draft of the Manifesto and a list of the scientists whom he was planning to ask to be signatories.

Einstein's last letter: "I am gladly willing to sign"

Ikeda: Russell's letter and Einstein's response have never been made public until now. I was very moved to receive from you the never-before-published correspondence that had been stored among reprints of the Manifesto. Einstein wrote, "Thank you for your letter of April 5. I am gladly willing to sign your excellent statement. I also agree with your choice of the prospective signers."

Rotblat: The unfolding of events from that point were truly dramatic. The date was April 18, 1955, and Russell was en route from Rome to Paris when he heard the announcement from the pilot of Einstein's death. Russell was very shocked and in despair. Without Einstein's signature, he thought, the announcement of the Manifesto would be less meaningful and lack authority and prestige.

When Russell arrived at his hotel in Paris, however, he found waiting for him a letter from Einstein that had been forwarded from London. In the letter were written the words that you, Dr. Ikeda, were just now reading regarding Einstein's intention to sign the Manifesto and his agreement on the list of other scientists who would be invited to sign.

Ikeda: This, then, was Einstein's last letter, written immediately before he died, which arrived after the news of his death had been announced. It is indeed his last will and testament to humanity. I feel that it is a very significant document.

Next, I would like to hear about your meeting with Lord Russell, who drafted the Manifesto. What kind of impression did he make on you?

Rotblat: Bertrand Russell was a man who always entertained new ideas. No one could imagine what was going through his mind. He would frequently astonish people with his wild ideas, but ultimately he would turn out to be right. For example, one of his sayings was, "Never be afraid of appearing eccentric, because" he said, "every idea which is now accepted, at the beginning seemed eccentric."

Ikeda: This is a very meaningful statement. It gives me a clear sense of Bertrand Russell as a man whose ideas are fresh and unique.

A powerful testimony, a special duty

Rotblat: The first time I met Bertrand Russell was a highly dramatic experience. It was right after the US had tested its first hydrogen bomb in March of 1954. The crew of a Japanese fishing vessel, the Lucky Dragon, which had been in nearby waters, was exposed to the radioactive fall-out when the wind changed direction, and one crew member died.

This was the incident that made the public aware of the hydrogen bomb. Up to that point, no one had known about its existence. As a result of this news, the BBC decided to broadcast a special program on the topic. This is a different broadcast from the Christmas broadcast that I mentioned previously. The program was a forum presenting differing opinions on the hydrogen bomb, and I participated as a member of the scientific community. The variety of participants included a military commander who stressed the military significance of the bomb and another person who pointed out its strategic value. Two other people debated the moral issues, and one of these individuals was Bertrand Russell.

In my discussion on the program, I tried to present in very simple terms the physics of the hydrogen bomb. Russell was apparently impressed by my description, and after the broadcast he told me that he had learned a great deal from my explanation. This was my first encounter with Lord Russell.

Ikeda: Interesting. Regarding the signatories to the Manifesto, eleven people signed, and one of them, Dr. Hideki Yukawa, was from Japan. My good friend, Professor Linus Pauling, was a signatory as well.

Rotblat: At the time the Manifesto was announced, all except two of the eleven signatories were Nobel Laureates. One of these two was Leopold Infeld from Poland. He was extremely active in the deliberations, and since he had collaborated with Einstein on several works on the theory of relativity, both Einstein and Russell wanted to include him as a signatory also.

The other person who was not a Nobel Laureate and who was the youngest of the group was myself. I pointed this out to Russell. I said, "Look, you are looking for Nobel Laureates, and I am not one." But he said, "You will be. You will be."

Ikeda: What a powerful testimony. He had marvelous foresight. And just as he predicted, you received the Nobel Peace Prize in 1995.

Rotblat: Yes, it did come to pass. And because I was the youngest of the eleven signatories, I am now the only one still alive. For this reason, I feel that I have been given a special duty. Actually, even more than a duty, I would say that it is more like a mission. I believe that my life's mission is to continue to convey the message of the Manifesto to everyone I can.

Ikeda: I was very moved and still am, even now, when I remember what you said when I met you in Okinawa in 2000. After our discussion I asked if you were tired, and you told me, "I can't afford to be tired."

Rotblat: That's because at that time, I was healthy and full of energy. To fulfill my mission to spread the message of the declaration, there were so many things that I needed to do that I didn't even have the luxury of being tired. However, on my ninety-fifth birthday, I suffered a minor stroke, and ever since my life has changed a little. I finally learned that no one is immortal. These days, I spend more time working at home rather than at the Pugwash office in the city. But even now, I receive a lot of phone calls, and every day is very hectic.

Ikeda: I heard that you had become ill, and I was worried about you. You are a treasure that we need in the twenty-first century. I am praying earnestly for your return to good health.

Rotblat: Thank you. And don't worry. I still have plenty to do to make sure that we are on the right track to achieve peace in the world.

A life dedicated to noble purpose

Ikeda: Professor Rotblat, you seem to be blessed with eternal youth. When a person awakens to his mission in life, he is youthful for his entire life. I recall that when Professor Linus Pauling, one signatory to the Manifesto and a distinguished scientist of the twentieth century, turned ninety years of age, he was still young in spirit.

I have unforgettable memories of when I spoke at Claremont McKenna College in Los Angeles, and Professor Pauling, then ninety-one years of age, came at short notice to serve as the panel commentator. Professor Pauling and I published a book of our dialogues. He is well known for his theory on the health benefits of vitamin C.

Rotblat: I have an interesting little story about that. One day, Linus Pauling came to my London office, and we had lunch together. At the time, I had a cold, so Linus asked me, "So, you have a cold, eh? Are you taking vitamin C?" I told him no. Then, he gave me a half-hour lecture on the health benefits of vitamin C and how the scientific data proved that vitamin C prevented colds. He convinced me, so I started taking vitamin C. Nine months later, when he came to visit, he asked me, "Are you taking your vitamin C?" I said yes, and he asked me how effective it had been. I told him that I had caught three colds this winter. To which he answered, "Is that so? How much have you been taking?" I told him that I had been taking 100 milligrams a day, just as he had told me, but he responded, "That's far too little. You have to take one gram a day."

Ikeda: That's an amusing little anecdote, and it sounds so much like Professor Pauling. I can just see him saying that.

In honor of his great contribution to science and peace, we at SGI held an exhibition cosponsored by the Pauling family and others, entitled "Linus Pauling and the Twentieth Century". The exhibition was wildly successful, attracting over a million people all around the world. Professor Rotblat, you came to the showing at the UN European Headquarters. Let me thank you again for coming.

Rotblat: I respected Professor Pauling greatly. He made an extremely valuable contribution to world peace. He and I worked together for many years. There is no doubt that he was one of the great people of my generation.

Encountering Einstein: tinsmith, peddler or lighthouse keeper

Ikeda: Next, please tell us about Albert Einstein. Did you ever meet Professor Einstein?

Rotblat: No, I didn't. This is because after World War II, I was considered a persona non grata by the United States. They thought I was a spy.

Ikeda: Wasn't this because, after your departure from the Manhattan Project, all kinds of suspicions followed you, and so, at that time, it was even more difficult for you to visit Einstein, who lived in the US?

Rotblat: That's right. They wouldn't let me into the country. I wanted to enter the US to visit Einstein and talk to him about the Manifesto, but the US government would not issue me a visa.

Ikeda: Great people always encounter persecution and slander. It seems to be a historical reality.

As we reflect on your past, it is apparent that your life was twice deeply affected by letters written by Professor Einstein. One was the letter Einstein wrote expressing his acceptance of Bertrand Russell's request to join him in becoming a signatory to the Russell–Einstein Manifesto. The other letter was one that Professor Einstein wrote to President Franklin D. Roosevelt, in which he called for the rapid development of nuclear weapons before the Nazis were able to do so. This letter became the major stimulus for initiating the Manhattan Project in which you participated.

Rotblat: Einstein was a self-declared pacifist. Therefore, it was totally unexpected for Einstein, the pacifist, to write a letter calling for the development of nuclear weapons. He explained his position in terms of accepting the fact that sometimes it may be necessary to fight for peace. For Einstein, a prominent scientist, to write such a letter meant that he had a profound understanding of the political environment and world in which he lived and was able to consider and accept ideas that were objectionable to others. For example, in the early 1930s, when Hitler came to power, Einstein understood the unimaginable horror that Hitler would inflict on the world. He could foresee, in the early period of the Hitler regime, that if Hitler were allowed to do as he wished, disastrous consequences would follow. It turned out that his predictions were accurate. He said, "We cannot allow Hitler to continue pursuing his plans. He must be stopped—with military means, if necessary."

Ikeda: Professor Einstein felt a responsibility to humankind that transcended ethnicity and nationality. And because he felt the anguish of humanity caused by war, he used his great talent and accomplishments to stand up for humanity on the issue of war and peace.

In the last years of his life, Einstein said that if he had to do it over again, he would have chosen a different profession such as tinsmith, peddler, or lighthouse keeper. One anecdote claims that, after hearing that the atomic bomb was dropped on the citizens of Hiroshima, Einstein cried out that if he had known that they were going to do that, he would not have become a scientist. We can only imagine the profound loneliness of such a heavy responsibility.

The profound loneliness of the dedicated pacifist

Rotblat: Of course, this great loneliness he must have felt was further compounded by the fact that Einstein was a pacifist who was urging the use of military force. If he had rigidly insisted on his own views, he would not have been able to take this position. But because he did, Einstein was called a traitor by peace activists and expelled from pacifist groups. He was criticized from all sides. Ultimately, however, it was shown that he was right. It turned out that his views were more correct than anyone else's. The lesson we can learn from this is that we must not be so inflexible that we insist only on our own principles.

Ikeda: The anguish that Einstein felt was closely linked with the question of whether there can be a "just war".

Bertrand Russell, who had opposed World War I and had been incarcerated for his views, supported World War II. He asked, "Are we to look upon Hitler's atrocities and do nothing?" We must be extremely cautious, however, about using the "just war" theory, which has been used frequently over the last sixty years to justify the use of force.

The atrocity of the Nazi Holocaust is symbolized by Auschwitz, and the Japanese have their own unjust invasion and the atrocities they committed in China and other Asian countries. The random bombing of Dresden, Tokyo, and Okinawa, as well as the dropping of the atomic bomb on Hiroshima and Nagasaki, are examples of atrocities committed by the Allied Forces.

The means must justify the ends, so we must not say that as long as the objective is true, then it can be achieved by any means. This leads us to the question of whether we can accept use of military force if the means are in balance and appropriate to the ends. This is basically the standpoint of the "just war" theory. But who will decide and what criteria will be used to determine whether or not a certain means is appropriate?

Just as you have insisted repeatedly, Professor Rotblat, the example of the atomic bomb during World War II indicates that once hostilities have begun, the first casualty is the ability for individuals or an entire society to make rational judgments. A sense of balance is lost to such a degree that an argument as absurd as allowing the killing of hundreds and thousands of people is accepted. We have already failed when violence and conflict cannot be resolved through nonviolent means. Even if it is necessary to use force to combat a foe who commits atrocities, we must be clear that killing another human being is just the same as brothers massacring each other. Of course, this was obvious to both Einstein and you, Professor Rotblat. Even so, if a conflict should require use of the atomic bomb, it would be an unimaginable situation. Despite holding this view, after the war the mass media vilified Einstein as the creator of nuclear weapons, and I imagine that this must have been unbearable for him.

Rotblat: Einstein felt that he did not have much to do with the actual development of the bomb. People say that the bomb resulted from the work of Einstein because they associate his famous formula, "$E=mc^2$" with the atomic bomb. This is from Einstein's theory of relativity and it means that under given conditions, mass (m) can be converted to energy (E) or vice versa. If you take mass "m", multiply it by the square of the speed of light (c), you get the energy of that mass. This is the formula that developed from his theory of relativity.

And so the atomic bomb is the first practical application of the formula. This means that the atomic bomb converts a small amount of matter in the atom into energy.

Ikeda: According to the formula "$E=mc^2$", as the speed of light in vacuum is 300,000 km per second, the energy will be "mass x 90,000,000,000". Just as a small stone is a lump of energy, human beings who are no more than small "thinking reeds", in Pascal's words, also have inherent within them an enormous latent cosmic power. Indeed, Einstein's formula gives us a glimpse into the dynamism and mystery of the laws of the universe. If using nuclear weapons is the manifestation of this power taken in an evil direction, then it should be possible to channel this power in a positive direction for good.

Rotblat: Einstein developed his formula not in order to make a bomb, but as a general principle of physics. For him, the formula was the product of pure scientific research. Even so, Einstein dreaded the consequences of the application of this principle. When Hitler came to power, there was no doubt that if he had had the bomb, he would have used it to subjugate the entire world. Einstein could not tolerate the thought of it. Therefore, he wrote a letter warning President Roosevelt of this possibility.

Einstein himself did not participate in the Manhattan Project. He refused to be a part of it, but he did send a second letter to President Roosevelt.

Ikeda: I believe you are referring to the letter he wrote in response to a request by Dr. Leo Szilárd in 1945. It urged the president to consider an international regulatory system to check the proliferation of nuclear weapons predicted by Dr. Szilárd.

Rotblat: Many people, including Einstein and other scientists, implored the president not to use the atomic bomb against the general public. But despite all these appeals, the bomb was ultimately used on civilians. In fact, once the military obtained the bomb, no matter how much scientists pleaded with them to spare innocent lives, the scientists no longer had any influence. They appealed to the military, saying, "Please don't use the bomb against human populations. Don't use the bomb at all. Just use it as a tool to threaten. Pretend that you will use it, but never actually use it."

The US military authorities turned a deaf ear to their pleas to prohibit the use of the bomb against civilians. In fact, as soon as the production was completed, the atomic bomb was used on Hiroshima and three days later on Nagasaki.

Ikeda: When he heard the news about the bombing of Hiroshima, Einstein was heard to say, "O weh!" a heart-rending cry in German, his native tongue. He was shocked beyond belief. That event, on that fateful day, drastically changed all of human history.

CHAPTER 6

From Hiroshima to Norway: Pugwash Wins the Nobel Prize

Ikeda: Professor Rotblat, you were awarded the Nobel Peace Prize in 1995. I am sure you have many thoughts on that experience, and so I would like to focus our discussion this time on that period in your life.

When you were the president of the Pugwash Conferences, I am told that your daily routine involved taking the bus and subway every morning from your home in the northern part of London, and arriving at your office before 9:00 am. When people would call the office, many of them would be surprised to hear your voice on the other end of the line.

The Pugwash Conferences for a long time had financial difficulties, and as president, you ran the organization without compensation. This did not keep you from tirelessly representing the nuclear abolition movement. For example, whenever you heard about an instance of nuclear weapons proliferation, you would immediately send a letter of protest to the country in question, and submit a letter to the editor of *The Times*, the leading English newspaper, and other mass media to declare your opposition.

Persuasion of the heart

Rotblat: The Pugwash Conferences organization is not a political pressure group, yet we believe that, as scientists, it is our mission and duty to warn humankind of the menace arising from the development of advanced scientific technology such as nuclear weapons. It is not as though we have a special strategy. Our weapons are words. That is, we are guided by discussion based on reason. We persuade our opposition with words, and this has been the basis of our peace movement.

Ikeda: Persuasion by words—I believe that dialogue impacts the human heart, and as the historian Arnold Toynbee concluded, indeed, it is the slow undercurrents that ultimately shape the landscape of history.

The intellectual contributions of Pugwash members as well as their extensive personal connections have been enormously helpful in attracting public support for a nuclear test ban as well as in establishing numerous military disarmament treaties.

Rotblat: Thank you. It does feel wonderful when our efforts are recognized. For example, we were truly gratified when former Russian President Mikhail Gorbachev expressed his appreciation for the Pugwash Conferences' contribution to military disarmament and the end of the Cold War.

I have devoted myself to working for peace for nearly sixty years, and am often asked how I was able to continue for so long. The major reason is that I believe, more than anything, in the goodness of human beings. Of course, when external forces are at work and outside pressure influences a situation, people may commit harmful acts. For example, in the early period of human history, humans fought and killed each other to protect their tribes and to compete for food, love, and women.

However, I believe that human beings are intrinsically good by nature. This has been my philosophy from the very beginning and is the principle that has enabled me to continue my fight for peace. In a sense, I am an optimist.

Ikeda: Professor Rotblat, your optimistic and steady approach resonates deeply with my philosophy. Peace activists are criticized for being unrealistic, and because they cannot always readily achieve their goals, they often lose the passion and vitality that they once had for their early ideals.

However, you, Professor Rotblat, have managed to hold on to your trust in human virtue and have persevered and continued your activities with a robust optimism. Former President Gorbachev's generous praise of your peace activities undoubtedly stems from his recognition of your profound and unwavering belief in the goodness of human nature.

Many people in Japan are inspired and heartened by your nuclear abolition activities. The first annual Pugwash Conferences General Assembly ever held in Japan was convened ten years ago.

Seized by a sense of shock in Hiroshima

Rotblat: Yes. It was held in 1995, fifty years after the nuclear bombs were dropped on Japan. At that time, nuclear proliferation was a growing concern, with China carrying on with its nuclear tests and France deciding to resume nuclear testing. In the midst of these developments, the Pugwash Conferences were held in Hiroshima—ground zero, you could say, of the movement.

In my address to the entire conference, I emphasized that, "The nuclear bombing of Hiroshima and Nagasaki was completely unnecessary. World War II could have been ended more quickly without dropping atomic bombs."

On the first day of the conference, when the conference participants visited the Memorial Cenotaph to offer flowers, I could not bring myself to leave the place for quite a while. This is because my heart was seized by the same sense of shock that I felt when I first heard the news of the dropping of the atomic bomb so long ago.

Many of the conference attendees encountered atom bomb victims for the first time, and for many of the Pugwash members, the annual assembly in Hiroshima invigorated them with renewed determination to work for the abolition of nuclear weapons.

Ikeda: What powerful and important testimony. Many of the world leaders that I have had occasion to meet tell me that they became much more aware of the menace of nuclear weapons after visiting Hiroshima and Nagasaki. I have consistently urged and will continue to urge all leaders of the nuclear powers to visit Hiroshima and Nagasaki to see for themselves what actually happened there. One can still see the lingering traces of tragedy that befell those cities. The historical significance of those two cities will never change.

The decision to recognize you and the Pugwash Conferences for your long years of efforts working for world peace and nuclear abolition came three months after the Pugwash general conference in Hiroshima. Where were you when you received notice that you had been awarded the Peace Prize?

Receiving the Nobel Peace Prize

Rotblat: I remember the day well. It was on Friday, October 13. I had gone to the office, as usual, and was working there. At about 11:00 am, the phone rang. Tom Milne, my secretary, answered the phone and said, "It's from Oslo." I knew immediately then that I had received the award. It was a call from an aide in the Norwegian legislature notifying me that I had been selected to receive the Nobel Peace Prize and that an official announcement would be made shortly. The call came forty-five minutes before the announcement.

I had known that I had been nominated, but since I felt that there was little chance for me, I was completely surprised. After hearing the news, I left the office for a walk, just as I usually do.

Ikeda: You took a walk?

Rotblat: Yes. I included a walk in my daily routine. I had to contemplate the consequences of this new development as I walked the streets of London. How would receiving the award influence my life? After giving this some thought, I came to a conclusion. I thought to myself, "I will not allow the Nobel Peace Prize to affect my life. I have so much that I still want to do. I must not allow this award to distract me from my goals."

Ikeda: Your words reflect a life of a great man who has fulfilled his mission while overcoming all difficulties. You have conquered the temptation to be distracted by criticism and praise, as expounded in a passage of Buddhist scripture: "Worthy persons deserve to be so called because they are not carried away by the eight winds: prosperity, decline, disgrace, honor, praise, censure, suffering, and pleasure."

Rotblat: I try. In any case, I went for a walk and when I returned to the office, the street in front of the building was filled with reporters and camera people. When I saw the crowd, I realized that it would not be easy to carry through my decision.

Ikeda: On that occasion, you commented that since the Nobel Peace Prize that was awarded to you and the Pugwash Conferences was for scientists who had devoted themselves to abolishing nuclear weapons, you hoped that many scientists would give more thought to the impact of their work on society. You also said, "My work is not yet finished", expressing your firm determination to continue your activities to bring about the abolition of nuclear weapons.

As you expressed, Professor Rotblat, you have continued your activities to this day and have not for an instant departed from your noble mission of nuclear abolition.

In May 2003, you kindly joined us at the "Linus Pauling and the Twenti-eth Century" exhibition that SGI held in Geneva at the UN European Headquarters, and at that time I heard that you told an SGI member, "I've been encouraged to write my memoirs, but I think it's a waste of time to reflect on the past. I still have a mountain of things I want to do."

You have such an active and forward-looking approach to life! I am determined to follow your example.

Rotblat: You are too generous. Likewise, I have great respect for you, Dr. Ikeda, and your persistent efforts for peace on the world stage.

When I found out that I had won the Nobel Peace Prize, I knew that I would never again be able to lead the tranquil and peaceful life that I had before. My premonition has turned out to be quite true indeed. For nearly ten years now, I have received more invitations to speak than I can accept. It is impossible to lead the life that I knew before.

I sometimes joke that since receiving the Nobel Peace Prize, I have turned into a less admirable human being. I say that because before I received the award, I would respond personally to every letter I received. If someone sent me an invitation, I would willingly accept. That is how I am. However, after receiving the Nobel Prize, it became humanly impossible to do as I did before.

Ikeda: Your comments reveal your honesty and upright character. The Sei-kyo Press reporter who interviewed you some time ago mentioned that he was impressed with your sincere manner.

Professor Rotblat, you are known for making sure that you personally confirm all the arrangements before each of the various international con-ferences that you are involved in planning. I am told that on the night before the conference held in Okinawa in 2000—sponsored by our Toda Institute of Global Peace and Policy Research—you came down to the con-ference auditorium to check the projector and microphone and were consulting amiably with the staff regarding the arrangements for the key-note speech you were going to deliver at the conference.

Rotblat: That's just my nature. But after receiving the Nobel Peace Prize, I became less and less able to live the way I want. For example, I receive hun-dreds of letters, and I can't answer them all by myself. I had to hire a secretary. So, Tom's brother came and has been writing replies for me. This is not ideal, and perhaps a little rude. I don't like to do things this way, but it can't be helped.

Also, it has become physically impossible for me to accept all the requests for speaking engagements. Even so, up until a year ago, I did as many of these engagements as I could. But then, I fell ill, and my life changed again. For medical reasons, my activities became very restricted. Now, I have to carefully consider my health and physical limitations when I decide what to do at work and when I travel to conferences.

"Remember your duty to humanity"

Ikeda: Professor Rotblat, you are the noble conscience of humanity and a precious world treasure. I sincerely wish for your good health and hope that you will continue to be involved in your activities.

Returning to our discussion of the Nobel Peace Prize, the Nobel Foundation made this statement in awarding the prize to you and the Pugwash Conferences:

> It is fifty years this year since the two atomic bombs were dropped on Hiroshima and Nagasaki, and forty years since the issuing of the Russell–Einstein Manifesto. The Manifesto laid the foundations for the Pugwash Conferences, which have maintained a high level of activity to this day. Joseph Rotblat was one of the eleven scientists behind the Manifesto and has since been the most important figure in the Pugwash work.
>
> The Conferences are based on the recognition of the responsibility of scientists for their inventions. They have underlined the catastrophic consequences of the use of new weapons. They have brought together scientists and decision-makers to collaborate across political divides on constructive proposals for reducing the nuclear threat.

It is my joy that your achievement has been recognized in this way and recorded in human history.

In December 1995, I was very moved by the acceptance speech that you delivered when you were awarded the Nobel Peace Prize in Oslo. It consisted of an overview of your philosophy of peace. I am wondering what you had in mind as you were delivering your talk.

Rotblat: I had a limited time period to speak, so I couldn't say all that I wanted. So, I decided to focus on several specific points. First of all, I considered the fact that the audience was made up of three types of people: government officials, scientists, and the general public. I appealed to their survival instinct, that is, I advocated for peaceful coexistence as the only way to enable humankind to survive. This was the central theme of my speech.

I addressed this issue to the governmental attendees in the following terms: "So I appeal to the nuclear powers to abandon the out-of-date thinking of the Cold War period and take a fresh look. Above all, I appeal to them to bear in mind the long-term threat that nuclear weapons pose to humankind and to begin action towards their elimination. Remember your duty to humanity."

Ikeda: Yours is an everlasting message to humankind. Professor Rotblat, as you have stressed for many years now, the nuclear deterrence theory, which contends that the existence of nuclear weapons will prevent war, is a fantasy. Unfortunately, however, even though the Cold War has been over for more than ten years, the nuclear powers still have not abandoned their nuclear weapons, claiming the need for "national security".

And now, not only is nuclear proliferation accelerating as India and Pakistan establish their nuclear programs, North Korea also is proceeding with development plans. Also, when we see movement toward nuclear proliferation such as in the case of the US, which is developing new forms of nuclear weapons, we should be very troubled that the Nuclear Non-Proliferation Treaty system, put in place to ensure nuclear weapons disarmament and non-proliferation, is confronting a major crisis.

Rotblat: I agree completely. And so, at the annual General Assembly of the Pugwash Conferences held in Korea in 2004, I warned: "While the nuclear powers are resisting talks to abolish nuclear weapons, the proliferation of nuclear weapons continues."

Ikeda: It's so true. In spite of the fact that five years ago [2000], the NPT Review Conference adopted a concluding statement that articulated the "commitments of the nuclear-weapon states to total nuclear disarmament", those efforts are not proceeding, and it is extremely regrettable.

If the nuclear disarmament process remains at a standstill, then leaders of the nuclear powers should be aware that the confidence of the international community in the NPT system will be shaken, and there will be increased danger not only of the proliferation of nuclear weapons, but also of biological, chemical, and other weapons of mass destruction.

Rotblat: I share your sense of alarm. When the terrorist attacks in the US on September 11, 2001 occurred, I expressed concern about nuclear weapons being used by the terrorists.

In addition to the responsibility of political leaders, I also emphasized the responsibility of scientists in my acceptance speech. I made an appeal to scientists based on my experience with the foolishness and cruelty inherent in the Manhattan Project.

> You are doing fundamental work, pushing forward the frontiers of knowledge, but often you do it without giving much thought to the impact of your work on society.
> Precepts such as "science is neutral" or "science has nothing to do with politics" still prevail. They are remnants of the ivory tower mentality, although the ivory tower was finally demolished by the Hiroshima bomb.

Ikeda: In your speech, you mentioned director Stanley Kubrick's movie *Dr. Strangelove or: How I Learned to Stop Worrying and Love the Bomb* [1964] as depicting the professional responsibility and conscience of scientists, and pointed to the shameful role that scientists played in inciting the arms race.

Rotblat: Yes. Since my youth, I have been passionate about science and have believed that science is the highest use of human intelligence. And I have always felt in my heart that science must be employed for the benefit of people. I would never have guessed that, ironically, I would spend the latter half of my life trying to protect humanity from the dangerous and foreboding threats of the products of science.

With these distressing thoughts in mind, I wanted to appeal to the world's scientists to not lose their humanity and conscience.

Ikeda: I understand your heartache and anguish. Fundamentally, science is neither good nor evil. It is the person using it that determines what it becomes. To that extent, the scientists on the leading edge of science must bear the heaviest responsibility.

Rotblat: Yes, that's true. Finally, at the end of my talk, I appealed to all the people of the world, because the resolute will and action of many people will be indispensable in building a world free of nuclear weapons and war.

I believe that it will be necessary to nurture a new kind of loyalty, to transform the loyalty of people toward the nation-state and to nurture in the heart of each and every person the consciousness of global citizenship and loyalty toward all humankind. So at the end of my talk, I delivered a call to action with the following words from the Russell–Einstein Manifesto: "We appeal as human beings to human beings: Remember your humanity, and forget the rest. If you can do so, the way lies open to a new paradise; if you cannot, there lies before you the risk of universal death."

Ikeda: That is a well-known passage. That spirit that has its origin in the Russell-Einstein Manifesto has survived ever since the founding of the Pugwash Conferences.

At the conclusion of your talk, I was touched by your broad appeal to the people of the world for a new awareness and sense of responsibility for manifesting global peace. I interpreted this as great encouragement for those of us who are struggling for world peace at the grassroots level. Also, this "loyalty toward all humankind" that you mentioned is a sentiment that has been expressed by Professor Arnold Toynbee. In a dialogue between Professor Toynbee and myself, he explained it in these terms: "My own paramount loyalty is to mankind, not to my local state and not to the establishment by which this state is controlled."[1]

He said that to confine state power to its proper and legitimate function, all humankind will have to be induced to give up its traditional quasi-religious devotion to nation-states.[2]

Rotblat: Of course, encouraging a sense of loyalty to all humankind does not mean that we would abandon loyalty to our countries. We all have a sense of belonging and loyalty to a variety of institutions from the family, which is the smallest group, to the nation-state, the largest group. Most important is that we not be bound by a narrow sense of loyalty. Rather, I believe that to overcome the problems and threats that cross borders and arise on a global scale, each individual must expand his or her sense of loyalty to humankind as a whole.

Ikeda: In my commemorative address delivered every year in January, I reiterate the importance of making the transformation to an era that serves the interests of all humanity and the earth, rather than the nation-state.

Karl Jaspers describes the circumstances in which modern man is placed:

> Modern man has to choose one way or another. Either he will fall into the abyss called "the loss of humanity" or "the loss of the human world", in other words, the standstill of human existence in general, or he will make a leap by a self-change to that which is intrinsically human or by a serendipitous opportunity for the intrinsically human to emerge.[3]

It is the ordinary people who should play the major role in this age. A great development will be made when each of them, with radiant humanity in their hearts, makes his or her effort to create and expand the web of human solidarity in order to erase the word "tragedy" from the world. This is the primary objective of the SGI "human revolution" movement in its endeavors in 190 countries and regions throughout the world.

CHAPTER 7

The Lie of Deterrence, the Vision of Abolition

Ikeda: Today, reductions in nuclear arsenals agreed upon by the nuclear powers are at a standstill, and the proliferation of nuclear weapons is becoming a very real crisis. Yet, despite this rapidly increasing menace, concern and passion for abolishing nuclear weapons is declining. This state of affairs is a grave cause for concern.

In our discussion this time, as we look back on the postwar nuclear age, I would like us to consider our next steps and discuss what specific means will help us truly manifest a world without nuclear weapons.

Rotblat: During the Cold War, the US and Soviet Union manufactured and stockpiled a massive amount of nuclear weapons. Recently, it was estimated that, at one point, the US nuclear arsenal alone equaled one million times the destructive power of the bomb dropped on Hiroshima. This is not only enough to destroy our civilization—it is more than enough to wipe out all of humankind. Indeed, one could say that the one distinctive feature of the nuclear age is that humankind now has the technology that would allow it, in a single act, to extinguish the entire human race.

In the short span of time since the bombing of Hiroshima and Nagasaki, an absurdly immense number of nuclear weapons have been amassed, and numerous times we have been on the verge of actually using them. Indeed, it would not be an overstatement to say that we have averted the ultimate catastrophe because of sheer luck and not because of a sophisticated crisis management system.

Whose peace? Why so many warheads?

Ikeda: I agree completely. Some people view the Cold War as having been won by the West or as having created the conditions necessary for a nuclear weapons strategy that helped maintain the peace. But these viewpoints seem biased.

First of all, in response to the claim that peace was maintained, I would ask, "Whose peace?" In reality, the system of nuclear deterrence has not been the guardian angel of peace that has prevented war. Rather, it has escalated the mistrust between East and West and has become a magnet drawing us toward conflict that has frequently erupted into proxy wars. For the peoples of the Korean peninsula, Indochina, and Central America, nuclear weapons have been the diabolical reason they have been pulled into war.

Second, during the Cuban missile crisis, which brought us to the brink of nuclear war, the deterrence theory proved false, and we now know that the situation was much more critical than was generally assumed at the time. According to Robert McNamara, then US secretary of state, also a member of the Canberra Commission, "We may have been wise, but to the same extent, we were blessed with good luck … ."[1] He also wrote, "The indefinite combination of human fallibility and nuclear weapons carries a very high risk of a potential nuclear catastrophe."[2]

In hindsight, one could say that the crisis was managed well, but there have been numerous other occasions that could have led to an inadvertent nuclear war. The most well-known instance in recent years occurred on January 25, 1995 when the Soviets mistook a Norwegian research rocket for a nuclear missile, and the Soviet president put into operation his "nuclear briefcase" for the first time.

Mr. Gorbachev determined to end the Cold War because, as the prime decision maker, he personally experienced the imminent danger of starting an inadvertent nuclear war.

I will always remember Mr. Gorbachev emphatically saying to me, "The world had arrived at a perilous brink. Any serious political collision could spark a nuclear war in which socialism, capitalism, and all ideological preferences and passions would go up in smoke."[3]

Rotblat: The issue that worries me the most today is that, for the majority of people, the fundamental consciousness about nuclear weapons has not changed at all. Political leaders, especially, still adhere to the notion that nuclear weapons are necessary to their national security. As long as nuclear weapons continue to exist, the threat of human extinction will always be like an axe held above our heads.

Ikeda: Today, over 30,000 nuclear weapons exist on the earth, and of those there are more than 12,000 strategic nuclear weapons.

Rotblat: I cannot, for the life of me, comprehend why it was necessary to have so many nuclear weapons. If the objective were mutual deterrence, one-hundredth of the current level would have sufficed. However, political policy required that the weapons continue to be manufactured—ostensibly for the purpose of deterrence, not offense.

The theory known as mutually assured destruction can be summed up in the brash claim, "If you attack us, you had better believe that we'll retaliate!" Possessing massive stockpiles of nuclear weapons to prevent mutual destruction is, of course, an extremely dangerous policy. It's based on a climate of mutual fear.

Ikeda: The acronym of mutually assured destruction is MAD, which means "crazy" in English.

Rotblat: Yes. It's very telling, isn't it? In the West, the idea is spreading that during the Cold War, nuclear weapons prevented a Soviet attack and averted World War III. This view has not been substantiated, however, in Soviet official documents, which have been obtained by Western historians. After the Cold War ended and the Soviet Union dissolved, the ideological conflict between the East and the West had been all but forgotten. In spite of this, the thinking of the past still lingers on and governs the policies of some countries.

Making the immoral illegal

Ikeda: Even though abolishing nuclear weapons is the rational course to take fundamentally, we cannot manage to do it. This is, as Einstein pointed out, a case of the world changing, but human thought remaining stuck in the past. One more economic factor must also be considered. There are groups today that stand to gain in the short term from the continuation of today's international military security arrangement that has allowed nuclear weapons to reach such proportions. This is a phenomenon described by former U.S. president Dwight D. Eisenhower as "the military–industrial complex".

Despite the immensity of the problem, it is becoming clear that citizens are raising their voices to advocate nuclear abolition, serving as a brake and establishing a base to support an international framework for nuclear disarmament.

Five years after the bombing of Hiroshima and Nagasaki, the US considered but abandoned the idea of using nuclear weapons during the Korean conflict. Even at that early date, the prevailing public opinion had an impact on the decision. During that same year, the Stockholm Appeal, seeking nuclear abolition, gathered 500 million signatures from around the world.

Rotblat: Since the beginning of the so-called nuclear age, there has been a universal, and forceful, call from all around the globe for the abolition of nuclear weapons. How did people react to the bombing of Hiroshima and Nagasaki? They were opposed to it because this new technology had an unfathomable destructive power, and even worse, they could witness for themselves the weapon's completely indiscriminate nature. Many people could tell, from the very beginning, that nuclear weapons were an immoral use of technology.

Even if nuclear weapons were technically legal, for example, there was the understanding their use should be prohibited on moral grounds. And so, it was agreed that the use of nuclear weapons was immoral, and a massive effort was launched to make them illegal.

Ikeda: Professor Rotblat, in order to advance the cause of nuclear weapons abolition, it is important not only to take a moral stand, but also to take a legal stand.

Rotblat: Yes. Perhaps not many people know that in January 1946, the first resolution at the first General Assembly of the United Nations was on the topic of nuclear abolition. As a result, a committee was established to deal with the problems arising from the discovery of nuclear energy. The UN membership was adamantly opposed to nuclear weapons from the very start.

The Nuclear Non-Proliferation Treaty, which took effect in 1970, gave the voices demanding nuclear abolition legal support. The signatories to the treaty included the five recognized nuclear powers, and this means that these countries are charged with the legal responsibility to advance the nuclear disarmament efforts of their own countries.

This treaty is composed of two primary components. One declares that no country should obtain, manufacture, design, or buy nuclear weapons. This means that the non-nuclear powers absolutely may not possess nuclear weapons.

The second component of the treaty applies to the five countries that already possessed nuclear weapons at the time of the ratification of the treaty. These nations were the US, the USSR, England, France, and China. Other countries were developing nuclear weapons, but they were not recognized as possessing them. One of these was Israel. India and Pakistan came much later. This brought the number of officially recognized nuclear powers to eight.

The second part of the treaty was designed for the eight countries, and dealt with nuclear disarmament. This is the most important part of the treaty.

Ikeda: You are referring to the sixth article, specifying the responsibility of the nuclear powers to conduct, in good faith, negotiations for nuclear disarmament.

In other words, the framework of the NPT indicates that in return for promising to abolish nuclear weapons, the non-nuclear countries would abandon their development of nuclear weapons. This also means that nuclear non-proliferation and nuclear disarmament are two aspects of the same effort. However, the reality is that the nuclear powers ignore or take Article Six lightly.

When the world's most powerful country violates a trust

Rotblat: Therefore, at the NPT review conference in 2000, the major nuclear powers were asked to make an unambiguous promise to abolish nuclear weapons. Yet, even though almost all the signatories agreed to abolish nuclear weapons, and specific objectives were established to realize this end, the current US administration seems to believe that the treaty assumes the continued existence of nuclear weapons. But this violates the treaty. In essence, the world's most powerful country is violating the nuclear disarmament treaty.

We live in a civilized society. Civilized society conducts itself according to laws. One set of laws applies to the domestic sphere, while another applies to the international sphere. Society as a whole is maintained because people observe these laws. So, when a treaty is signed, adherence is required.

Ikeda: Looking back on the movement to abolish nuclear weapons, the NPT review conference in 2000 to clarify the major powers' commitment to nuclear disarmament revealed that major progress has been achieved during the past decade, through such efforts as the movement in the nineties to establish the illegality of nuclear weapons.

Advances are evident in such developments as the cautionary opinion of the International Court of Justice, which rules that "the threat or use of nuclear weapons would generally be contrary to the rules of international law applicable in armed conflict, and in particular the rules and principles of humanitarian law"(July 1996), the adoption of the Comprehensive Nuclear Test Ban Treaty (CTBT)(September 1996), and the establishment of regions declaring themselves to be "nuclear-free zones".

After the terrorist attacks of September 11, 2001, however, the world became engulfed in a circle of violence between terrorists and anti-terrorist retaliation. And while there is a great hue and cry about the menace of nuclear proliferation and the cooperative activity between terrorists and "rogue states", nothing has been said about reducing the massive nuclear arsenals of the nuclear powers. This unfair and warped international order ultimately serves as a breeding ground for new terrorists.

Rotblat: My view of the relationship between terrorism and nuclear weapons is that nuclear terrorism is an extension of the policy of nuclear deterrence, the reason being that "nuclear deterrence" is the ultimate form of terrorism. In other words, one is prepared to use nuclear weapons in support of one's own political views and philosophy. And this is indeed terrorism.

Upon reflection, this means that, if the occasion ever arose, leaders of countries, whether Vladimir Putin or George W. Bush, have to have the psychological makeup that would enable them to press the button that would destroy the world. To my mind, this, too, is a form of terrorism.

Ikeda: Now, the word "terrorism" is used to refer to violence committed by groups that are "non-state actors", but is derived from the reference to "government through fear", as practiced by Robespierre during the French Revolution. And so originally, the word "terrorism" was used to refer to violence perpetrated by governmental authorities.

I am reminded of the story of Alexander the Great, told by the Roman Emperor Augustine. When Alexander scolded pirates terrorizing the seas, the pirates said, "Since I do this with a little ship I am called a pirate. You do it with a great fleet and are called an emperor."[4]

In any case, as many people, including UN Secretary-General Kofi Annan, have expressed, after the September 11 terrorist attacks, the word "terrorist" has come to be used in an overly simplistic way and, at times, tends to be abused in a strategic effort to obscure other important issues.

When policies depend on violence

Rotblat: That terrorism is spreading to such an extent throughout the world is the direct result of policies that are dependent on violence. If we are to combat terrorism, we must begin to nurture a culture of peace, not the strategy followed by the US.

We often tell young people not to choose violence. However, young people can see that we are attempting to achieve peace through the most evil weaponry ever invented by man. This mindset ultimately nurtures a culture of violence.

Ikeda: I agree. We really must think more seriously about how we have created a culture of war. For many years in the Third World, we trampled on people's dignity with violence that is both direct, as in the violence perpetrated by colonial rule, as well as indirect and structural, through the debilitating impact of poverty and inequality.

Resentment and dissatisfaction are the root cause of terrorism in today's world. If we continually focus on religious conflict and the clash of cultures, we may misinterpret the problem. Of course, terrorism should never be excused, and an international framework to prevent terrorism should be put in place. This alone, however, is only a partial solution and not a way to reach a fundamental resolution. The other half of the solution should be to address the conditions that give rise to terrorism in the first place. This would involve creating a world founded on the principles of equality and coexistence.

As a first step toward achieving such a world, the danger of nuclear weapons and the associated potential for human extinction should be eliminated. You and the Pugwash Conferences have built up a valuable store of research and analysis to reach this goal. I would like to ask you, Professor Rotblat, if you think that nuclear weapons can really be abolished, and if so, how can this be done?

Canberra Commission: why and how to abolish nuclear weaponry

Rotblat: In 1990, right after the fall of the Berlin Wall, the Pugwash Conferences conducted research on creating a world without nuclear weaponry, and the results of this research were presented in 1993 in the report *A Nuclear-Weapon-Free World: Desirable? Feasible?*[5] Other people have done research, including a comprehensive study conducted at a number of prestigious research institutes such as the Henry L. Stimson Center in Washington, DC and the Committee on International Security and Arms Control of the US National Academy of Science. Also adding weight to the efforts are the International Court of Justice opinion and the Statement on Nuclear Weapons by International Generals and Admirals, composed of sixty individuals from seventeen countries.

Among these statements, the most important is the Canberra Commission's report released in August 1996. The Commission's report asked the question "Why must we abolish nuclear weapons?" and then proceeded to consider the question "How can nuclear weapons be abolished?"

Ikeda: You were one of the seventeen members of the Commission. The Canberra Commission's report stood in the world's spotlight.

Rotblat: The first two proposals dealt purely with the military aspects of the issue. In other words, it discussed taking nuclear forces off a state of alert and removing warheads from delivery devices. These measures dramatically reduce the danger of an unauthorized or inadvertent launch of nuclear weapons. They can be accomplished relatively quickly if we decide to do so.

The third proposal was to end deployment of non-strategic nuclear weapons. The fourth proposal was to terminate nuclear testing. The fifth proposal was to initiate negotiations to reduce US and Russian nuclear weapons capability.

In the final proposal, the Canberra Commission sought agreement for a non-first use policy and for a general principle of non-use. In my opinion, this is the most important step toward total abolition of nuclear weapons.

If this agreement holds, then a fundamental change would be made to today's nuclear policy, which is based on the claim that nuclear weapons are necessary to act as a deterrent against attacks from non-nuclear states, and a major obstacle would be overcome.

It would not be an overstatement to say that this principle of non-first use, in the form of a so-called "negative security assurance", is actually what is already in effect. At the 1995 NPT Review and Extension Conference, the nuclear powers reaffirmed their position on non-first nuclear strikes against any of the signatories of the NPT regime. However, this assurance came with a number of delimiting factors, which made it of little value. Moreover, this assurance was granted by the nuclear powers, which means that it could just as easily be revoked.

Ikeda: Yes. I believe that it is just as you fear. As we can see in the US Nuclear Posture Review, a move is afoot in this modern international society to justify the continued use of nuclear weapons as more "usable weapons".

Rotblat: Russia has also abandoned the non-first use policy that the former Soviet Union declared. This state of affairs calls for, as I have been insisting, a non-first use of nuclear weapons treaty, rather than the current voluntary statements of individual countries.

Ikeda: Yes, I agree. However, some insist that nuclear abolition is "unrealistic", because once people have the technology, they will never give it up. And even if nuclear weapons are abolished, there will be people who will want to develop the capability. Therefore, abolition is unrealistic. How do you respond to this argument?

Rotblat: The argument supporting nuclear abolition, summarized in the Canberra Commission report, is not easily assailed. Consequently, the supporters of nuclear weapons have shifted the argument. They argue that a world free of nuclear weapons will not be safe. Even if a treaty that abolishes nuclear weapons is concluded and implemented, they say there is no guarantee that the treaty will not be violated.

Borrowing from popular culture, they say that once the genie has escaped from Aladdin's magic lamp, it can never be put back inside. Of course, we can never erase the knowledge of how to create nuclear weapons. And even if we create a world without nuclear weapons, no one can guarantee that some country at some future date will not deploy nuclear weapons to intimidate its neighbors and make the entire world kneel at its feet.

This argument, however, is no reason not to prohibit nuclear weapons. If you accept this reasoning, then we would oppose every disarmament measure and treaty. One counterargument is the example of the Chemical

Weapons Convention (CWC), which went into effect in April 1997. Knowledge of chemical weapons manufacture, as in the case of nuclear weapons, cannot be eradicated. It would be easier to reproduce chemical weapons than nuclear weapons. Yet, we concluded a treaty prohibiting chemical weapons.

A precedent: keeping advanced technology unused

Ikeda: Also, I would like to point out that even if the knowledge cannot be eradicated, it is conceivable that the knowledge would just not be utilized. During the sixteenth century period of warring states, Japan possessed the world's most advanced firearms technology. However, the Tokugawa regime that took control in the following Edo period managed the manufacture of firearms and gunpowder and made the decision to return to the culture of the sword. As a result, a peaceful period of over 200 years ensued.

Although a different time and social context, this is one example of an advanced technology that was kept unused and intentionally retired at one point in time. Nuclear weapons, as the label "weapons of mass destruction" suggests, are weapons that differ so much in scale from other weapons that they are a manifestation of evil itself. Because we view them as so different, however, we must not fall into the trap of believing that they cannot be abolished. Once we decide that we can do it, a firm resolve and a strong will are all that are necessary to succeed.

In a world in which nuclear weapons are illegal, possessing them would be considered a shameful act. For example, imagine if a country wanted to revive slavery and the system of apartheid today. It would incur criticism from the entire world and invoke sanctions against it. Even so, as you say, there is no guarantee that after nuclear weapons are banned, no one will try to reproduce them. For this reason, an important key will be the kind of inspection system that is put in place.

Effective surveillance of nuclear treaty violations

Rotblat: You are absolutely right. Just as in the case of the treaty to ban chemical weapons, one would expect to introduce a strict inspection system to minimize the potential for treaty violations. A variety of studies into the nature of this system are already being conducted. Of course, there is no system that can claim to be 100 per cent failsafe.

Furthermore, in a world without nuclear weapons, there is no guarantee of complete security. But at least we can aim to create a world that is more secure than one with nuclear weapons. This is entirely within the realm of possibility.

Ikeda: What kind of surveillance and inspection system do you have in mind?

Rotblat: It would be a two-tiered system. One tier is technological in nature. It would enable inspection and verification by remote technologies. For the other tier, I recommend a "societal inspection system". By adopting this other little-known means, the potential for successfully ensuring a nuclear weapons ban would be even greater. In this societal inspection system, not only the experts but also all citizens and members of the entire community would work to ensure the effectiveness of the nuclear weapons ban treaty.

From a legal perspective, a nuclear weapons ban treaty would establish the following strategy. Domestic laws would be enacted that would make it the right and responsibility of all citizens of signatory countries to report any violations of the treaty to the international authorities.

Ikeda: I see. By enacting domestic laws, a citizens' "nuclear watch" system would be established that would be more thorough and reliable.

Rotblat: That is correct. In this societal inspection system, citizens will play the role of inspectors, and scientists will be especially important. For rogue states and terrorist groups to develop nuclear weapons, they have to set up an experimental laboratory equipped with special instruments—a task that would be impossible without the assistance of a scientist with specialized knowledge.

The same also would be true for other sciences and technological fields. If research is being conducted that is harmful to society, it is a scientist's responsibility to expose it. The responsibility to report this type of information, anonymously or otherwise, should be part of a scientist's ethical code of conduct. I propose that when a scientist informs on activities dangerous to society, that act should be legally protected and the penalty for divulging classified information should be waived.

Ikeda: So you are saying that it is essential that we create an environment in which scientists as well as all members of society can remain faithful to their consciences. In order for this to happen, first of all, it is important that each person take action based on firm convictions and a code of ethics. For that purpose, civil education and accurate information access and delivery will be needed above all.

Second, laws must be enacted that provide incentive and protect such actions.

Rotblat: I believe that, given the political will and ability to implement the proposals we have discussed thus far, we should be able to abolish or put a complete ban on the use of nuclear weapons within twenty or thirty years. If such a scenario comes to pass, the threat of nuclear war will be greatly reduced. The reason that I say, "greatly reduced" rather than "eliminated" is that we cannot absolutely guarantee that, in the future, someone will not stockpile nuclear weapons and create a situation that forces us back into another Cold War.

Another thought to consider is that there may be other technologies that could potentially drive humankind to extinction. How, then, are we to ensure the continuity and survival of the human race? The answer is self-evident: all the fundamental threats to humankind come from war, so we must stop waging war. In other words, the best way to avert catastrophe is none other than to abolish war itself.

Many people think that the idea of a world without war comes from an imaginary, fanciful, and unrealistic view of the world. Even people who support the vision of a world without nuclear weapons would probably agree that to hope for a world of countries without war-waging capabilities is unrealistic.

Yet, in Europe, where historically war was equivalent in impact to endemic disease, the majority of countries, including some that were mortal enemies in the past, belong to the European Union. Now, when conflicts arise, no one would think of resolving them militarily. In other parts of the world, we see military dictatorships crumbling and democratic governance has become the only model. A major feature of this age is an increasing recognition of the meaninglessness of war and a pure desire on the part of people to avoid military conflict.

Nonviolence: humanity's common goal

Ikeda: Yes, I agree. The unity of the European Union, for example, was made possible by a staunch political will and the desire of the populace for a world in which never again would countries inflict the tragedy of war on each other.

As Blaise Pascal once said, "And thus being unable to make what is just strong, we have made what is strong just."[6] Heretofore, the tone of human history probably was based on the ethic of power, that is, the powerful called the shots and exerted their control over the weak. In this context, it undoubtedly appeared, at times, unrealistic to advocate an end to violence and war. However, with the development of information science, solidarity for nonviolence among citizens has become a reality worldwide.

The International Campaign to Ban Land Mines that produced the Mine Ban Treaty (also known as the Convention on the Prohibition of the Use, Stockpiling, Production and Transfer of Anti-Personnel Mines and on Their Destruction) is an excellent example of how the will of peace-seeking people evolved into a mainstream movement.

4. "Nuclear Arms: Threat to Our World" exhibit by Soka Gakkai, 1996.

I believe that we are beginning to see a major historical trend in world public opinion in favor of a world without war. This is something that must happen.

The preeminent poet Tagore expresses this thought. He wrote, "Very often it is mistakes that require longer time to develop their tangles, while the right answer comes promptly."[7]

We are now in an age in which we should boldly shout out to the entire world these clear and truthful messages "No more nuclear weapons!" and "Put an end to war!"

CHAPTER 8

Science and Faith: The Extension of Reason

Ikeda: You say that unprecedented and staggering changes have occurred in the lives of humankind during the twentieth century, driven largely by developments in science.

Rotblat: That is exactly right. The twentieth century could well be called the era of the "explosion of science".

Ikeda: While acknowledging the immense contributions of science to humanity, you cast the bright light of truth on its dark underside. A symbol of this negative underside of science is the atomic bomb, which you have spent much of your life fighting to abolish.

Professor Rotblat, you have frequently pointed out that science divorced from the responsibility of the scientist is unthinkable. In our conversation now, I would like to delve into this issue a bit further.

Rotblat: First of all, let me provide a general perspective on the meaning of "responsibility". By "responsibility", I am referring to the social responsibility held by all people, not only scientists. As members of society, each one of us belongs to some kind of group. In contemporary society, it is impossible for anyone to live a completely isolated life. Indeed, life as we know it is made possible by the assistance of others.

Understanding one's debt to others

Ikeda: I believe that this is called "interdependence". Our lives are made possible by the help and hard work of many people, including our forebears, whose legacy we enjoy. It is important for us humbly to acknowledge this reality.

Rotblat: We contribute to the groups in which we take part, and this makes our lives more efficient. If we were to live in isolation, we would have the sole responsibility of taking care of everything related to our maintenance and survival, such as hunting, growing food, and searching for fuel to provide warmth. This would be impossible.

Each of us has our own roles and areas of expertise. Some people make clothes, some grow vegetables, and others study religion. And so we live our lives by cooperating with each other, being considerate of each other, and contributing in a variety of ways to the groups to which we belong. Every one of our lives benefits from, and indeed is enriched by, the contributions of others.

Ikeda: In oriental culture, this notion is expressed in terms of "gratitude". "Understanding one's debt" to others is a primary condition for membership in the human race. To forget one's debt to another is shameful.

It is arrogant for a person to think that he has no one to thank for the many blessings he enjoys in his life. In his work entitled, *The Revolt of the Masses*, the Spanish author José Ortega y Gasset identified this characteristic of individuals today with the well-known expression, "*señorito satisfecho*" (self-satisfied young man).[1]

One need only look around to realize that we are dependent on others all around the globe. At the beginning of the twentieth century, the first president of Soka Gakkai, Tsunesaburo Makiguchi, had already realized this and written about it in his masterwork, *The Geography of Human Life*. He wrote:

> I am from a poor village in Arahama in northern Japan, an ordinary man who has spent half of his life pursuing daily necessities, making little contribution to the world outside. However, when I consider the things surrounding me, I am astonished at the broad origins of the objects that affect my life. For example, a piece of wool cloth wrapped around my body was originally produced in South America or Australia and processed in England by the labor of British people and with coal and iron mined there. My shoes have soles made from leather produced in the United States, and the rest of the shoe is made from leather produced in India. On my desk is a kerosene lamp; it is silent, though the oil inside it might well be saying, 'I sprang from the foot of the Caucasus Mountains along the coast of the Caspian Sea and arrived here after traveling thousands of miles.' My glasses have lenses produced with skill and precision by people in Germany ... It will be easier for us to perceive the

extent of our interrelations with the larger world around us if we recognize the presence of such relationships in even the smallest aspects of an ordinary person's life.[2]

Rotblat: Your example establishes quite clearly the link between our daily lives and other people around the globe.

Ikeda: Yes. If we think in these terms, we can understand how we exist in relationships of interdependence and mutual assistance with the rest of the world. Every other person alive is indispensable to our own existence.

Lighting a lamp for others

Rotblat: You are entirely correct. I would like to suggest here that if we are dependent on the assistance of others, in turn, we are then obligated to assist others as well. In other words, "responsibility" is not an issue only for scientists, but all citizens have a responsibility for their actions. This is the fundamental principle on which society is based.

The interdependence of all humanity has in recent years progressed rapidly with the advance of technology. Telecommunications have made interaction between people extremely simple. Simultaneously, our responsibility towards others, that is, our social responsibility, which each person must fulfill, has grown heavier.

It behoves us to be considerate of others, because in the end, we benefit. This is one of the fundamental precepts of civilization. If we cannot observe this simple truth, we may as well return to the life of primitive cave dwellers during the Stone Age.

Ikeda: Professor Rotblat, you express very succinctly a critical maxim. The Buddhist scriptures state, "If one gives food to others, one will improve one's own lot, just as, for example, if one lights a lamp for another, one will brighten one's own way."[3] In today's world, however, it seems that this sentiment has waned considerably. I believe that this is a root cause of many of the social problems that we face.

Rotblat: I agree. When I say that scientists have a special responsibility, I am referring to the increasing impact of science on society. The consequences of scientific development and its application in society over the last one hundred years have completely changed the nature of our lives.

Scientists bear a special responsibility for giving birth to new ideas, new lifestyles, and new material goods.

The development of weapons of mass destruction has made exercising this responsibility urgently necessary. After all, we have now acquired the capability of destroying human civilization itself.

Ikeda: As Albert Einstein so keenly discerned, unleashing the power of the atom has changed everything but our modes of thinking. This is why it is even more necessary to make a major effort to transform our sense of values and understanding of spirituality.

Rotblat: I concur completely. For the first time in human history, we have the technological means to quite literally wipe ourselves off the face of the earth. This is largely the result of the work of scientists.

This fact must be constantly reiterated. But even now, many scientists feel that the application of their work is none of their business and that they are committed to conduct scientific research for the sake of science. Some scientists may say, "We have the capability to make bombs that can destroy all the cities of the world, but how these bombs are used is no concern of mine. That is for others to decide." I believe that this is an immoral attitude. Yet today, many scientists think this way.

Distinguishing between knowledge and wisdom

Ikeda: This is an enormous problem. The critical point is that we must think in terms of how the knowledge that humankind possesses can be used to further human happiness. Needless to say, we must seek diligently the wisdom to accomplish this goal. Knowledge and wisdom may seem similar, but they are derived from completely different spheres. In other words, because we have expanded our volume of knowledge, we cannot say that we have necessarily grown wiser.

Our second president and my teacher and mentor, Josei Toda, once said that one of the greatest misunderstandings of modern civilization is this confusion between knowledge and wisdom.

The Buddhist scriptures refer to the "talented animal".[4] No matter how much knowledge and talent a person possesses, without morality or ethical principles to restrain one's desires, major misfortune will result.

Rotblat: I agree completely with Mr. Toda's distinction between knowledge and wisdom. They are both extremely important, but certainly not synonymous. I am not sufficiently knowledgeable about animal behavior and could not discuss this in terms of the social behavior of animals. However, I do believe that we can consider the distinctions in the context of human society. As we have so often seen, possession of knowledge does not necessarily mean that we know how to use it.

Suppose that we invent a new tool. This capability would be called "knowledge". The understanding of how to use the tool is an issue of wisdom. The question of how to use knowledge requires wisdom. Knowledge itself is extremely important. Without it, progress is impossible. However, knowledge alone is insufficient. We must know how to apply this knowledge.

The world's scientists can make a definitive statement about the application of scientific knowledge in society because they have had such an immense impact on people's lives and have played a major role in shaping contemporary society.

Ikeda: I cannot possibly put into words my thanks for your confirmation of the very points my mentor instilled in us. Humankind has amassed an enormous store of knowledge over the course of our long history. However, can we really say that we have grown commensurately wiser with the passage of time? Wisdom cannot be bequeathed to succeeding generations the way knowledge can be passed down, because it can only develop through the knowledge gained by living and through cultivating one's character. This is the foundation on which human beings create value and thereby seek to build a peaceful world that ensures the happiness of all people.

Professor Rotblat, what do you think is most essential for humankind to develop and deepen our wisdom? Also, what kind of wisdom will be required for us to meet successfully the challenges of the new age that we face?

Rotblat: Up until this point, I have witnessed numerous examples of the mistaken and misguided use of knowledge. Especially in the twentieth century, humankind created horrible and terrifying new inventions.

Let us examine the German example. In the first half of the twentieth century, Germany was already a highly developed civilized country. Germans were well educated and possessed an abundance of technical knowledge. However, in spite of their considerable knowledge, they permitted Nazism to develop and take over their country. They voted for Hitler, who—in spite of his anti-scientific ideas—was able to acquire political power and implement his program of mass murder of Jews, discriminating against them based on racial background. Moreover, all of this was accomplished in a highly scientific and systematic way.

Millions of Jews were massacred in the German gas chambers. Never before in human history had such atrocities been committed on such a massive scale.

Ikeda: This is an extremely difficult lesson of the twentieth century.

Rotblat: When confronted with such horrifying facts, can we really say that we have become more civilized with the passage of time? Have we not become more animal-like in our behavior? Perhaps this claim would be an insult to the animal kingdom. Rather, it may be more accurate to say that this reveals a complete lack of any moral consciousness. This is what we have witnessed during the twentieth century.

I am sure that you are often told never to forget the tragedies of Hiroshima and Nagasaki. To this I would also add, we must never forget the millions of lives lost in the Chechen war and in the gas chambers in Poland. This was the forced incarceration and mass murder of millions of innocent victims who just happened to belong to a specific racial group.

Ikeda: It is a terrible thing. Nothing like this must ever happen again.

Raising the quality of education to the humane level

Rotblat: My sentiments exactly. If I may, I would like to tell you a wartime story. A scientist was doing "scientific" experiments to determine how long a person could remain underwater without taking a breath. He used human beings as guinea pigs. That kind of practice should never again be permitted. It follows that education is of ultimate importance. Whatever the issue, the answer seems always to point to the necessity for education.

A person capable of doing such an experiment could not have received an education in the true sense of the word. This kind of person is one that is easily swayed by what others say, and accepts unquestioningly the nonsense of ideologies such as Nazism. To avoid these tragedies again, a higher quality education must be offered.

Ikeda: This is the only way. The Dutch humanist, Erasmus, pointed out, "Education exerts such a powerful influence, as Plato says, that a man who has been trained in the right develops into a sort of divine creature, while on the other hand, a person who has received a perverted training degenerates into a monstrous sort of savage beast."[5]

In contemporary society, most essential to managing our highly sophisticated knowledge base are an evolved wisdom, ethics and the strength of character to discipline the self. To this end, I believe that a humanistic education is vitally important, and accordingly, I have put all my efforts into helping to develop an outstanding humanistic education. Nothing is more detrimental than an education that lacks the intention to cultivate one's character.

Rotblat: In my opinion, the gap between the haves and the have-nots is expanding. Yet, I believe that little by little, young people are receiving a higher quality education. Even if progress is being made a little at a time, the level of human education is rising. This is why I still believe that there is hope.

Ikeda: There is no question that the role of education is to cultivate human beings. At the same time, I cannot help but think about the role of religion as I observe the various phenomena in contemporary society that manifest a pathology characterized by an absence of humanity.

I believe that religion can play a critical role in reviving and radiating a sense of humanity in people's hearts. It is also true that historically, religion has deviated from its fundamental spirit and been used by political power. It has served as a dividing force and source of conflict between people. The essence of many tragic scenarios shows a reversal in the role of religion, that is, revealing religion not as an entity existing to benefit people, but rather, as an entity that uses people for its own ends.

Religion: aid or abuse?

Rotblat: This is a field that I find most difficult to address. Religion comes to the aid of people in their daily lives, while at the same time it is frequently abused when people try to force their own opinions on others. Since medieval times, religion has been used adeptly by the upper strata of society to stigmatize those whose opinions were offensive and contrary to the accepted religious dogma. This same perspective can be seen in the doctrines and rhetoric of certain extreme schools of fundamentalist Islam.

Of course, religious wars have also occurred. Many of the wars were international in scope and raged over a long period of time. One example is the conflict between the Catholics and the Protestants in Northern Ireland.

Sadly, generally speaking, it seems to me that when people are educated to a certain point, religion seems to create more harm than good. But, of all the religions, Buddhism seems to be the least harmful to people.

Ikeda: I can see examples of exactly what you are saying in the history of religion in Europe. For instance, as we saw in Japan, if members of the clergy are derelict, the society is negatively impacted. Without the illumination that comes with development of the intellect, the danger is that religion and faith lacking in rationality and conscience will turn into "blind faith".

I believe that education and religion are inseparable sides of the same coin that nurtures a profound spirituality, cultivates human potential, and enhances a sense of humanity in individuals.

Rotblat: I am a scientist and, as such, I am accustomed to seeking rational explanations for everything. During my life, I have observed the development of concepts such as the origins of life, and examined them from a purely rational perspective using natural scientific and physical laws. In my observations, I have never come across anything that I cannot sense with my own powers of perception, that is incongruous with any physical law, or that suggests evidence of the existence of anything of a supernatural nature.

But that said, I am not so attached to my own ideas that I think that I am always correct in everything I do or say. I do not deny that phenomena that I cannot understand could be explained by divine power. But, as a scientist, all I am saying is that I have to eliminate the possibility of the existence of God, because I have insufficient evidence.

I have to admit, however, that there are really many things that I do not know. I am not a particularly religious person, and this is the reason for my agnosticism. To be an agnostic simply means that I do not know and will keep seeking the answer for eternity. This is my response to questions about religion.

Ethics or extinction

Ikeda: It is a very sincere response. I believe that true religious faith does not contradict reason. Indeed, sound reasoning seeks true faith, and true faith illuminates the highest rationality. Albert Einstein once said, "Science without religion is lame, religion without science is blind."

Basically, both religion and science are a means to explore the universal laws that underpin all of creation, including our own human existence. Therefore, if scientists and religious adherents can cooperate to help build a code of ethics for global citizenship, they will have made an invaluable contribution. And of course, a code of ethics for scientists will become an even greater issue.

Rotblat: I recognize a role for religion, but I view it from the standpoint of the evolution of an ethical standard created by global citizens. By this I mean "natural evolution". In other words, everything is in a state of constant change. Humankind also has continued to change over the past billions of years.

Change manifests itself, in time, even in entities with an extremely low probability of change. Generally speaking, evolution will proceed in a beneficial direction. For example, life is this way, human beings, animals, or any kind of organisms can evolve in any direction.

Evolution can take two paths. A species could thrive if the evolutionary process makes it hardy, or on the contrary, it could become weak. If the species grows weaker, it will decline and become extinct. Accordingly, the species that survive through the evolutionary process are the only ones that have grown stronger. This is why the evolutionary process is a beneficial one.

Ikeda: Through evolution, all living things are subjected to natural selection.

Rotblat: Yes. Therefore, I contend that the evolutionary process itself is the foundation of ethics. This is to say that the stronger a species, the finer the final product. Viewed over the long term, we should be able to make progress toward higher ethical principles through the developmental process of evolution. If we hope to survive, we have to strive for goodness. If we do not, we will surely become extinct. This is my own philosophy and the basis for my ethical code.

Ikeda: I see. Today, the specter of human extinction is no longer a remote possibility, and herein lies the reason to shout out with all one's might about the imperative to develop a code of global ethics that will ensure societal harmony and coexistence.

Professor Rotblat, your philosophy includes your profound trust in human goodness and an infinite faith in the human intellect.

Rotblat: I believe in science and technology. As I mentioned to you earlier, since childhood, I have been deeply impressed by the possibilities of science. The potential of science is limitless and universal. This is why science has been able to solve humankind's difficulties.

People are not oriented to go to war. We are not biologically programmed with a soldier's mentality. Some say that this is part of our genetic makeup, but I do not believe that this is the case at all. This is why I believe that science will eventually discover the means to nurture all people. No matter how much the earth's population increases, I believe that science will provide enough food and resources to make it possible for all the people in the world to coexist together peacefully. This is my basic philosophy of science and life.

Technology: agent of polarity or transcendence?

Ikeda: I am well aware of the depth of your expectations for the future of science as well as the value you place on the conscience of scientists.

Human beings have the goodness of heart to love and care for others deeply, but they also have another side that is destructive and self-centered. Buddhism holds a profound insight into human nature, and offers a profound philosophy and practice in daily life to develop and nurture human virtue.

In Soka Gakkai International, we teach a process of "human revolution", based on the principles of Buddhist law, which aims to bring about a transformation of the individual as well as society. In any case, there is no greater value than the dignity of life. Thus, the point of departure from which the progress of humankind springs is this indispensable idea of "dignity of life".

Rotblat: Yes, I agree. I think that in the next several decades, some major changes that transcend national borders will occur in the international community. In the field of science and technology, the application of biotechnology and telecommunications technology, in particular, will change society greatly.

These changes have the potential to go in two different directions. One of them is an increasing polarization known as the "digital divide" in which the upper strata of society will become increasingly blessed with the benefits of using new technology, and the lower classes become increasingly left behind.

In contrast, another scenario is that all the people of the world will recognize their membership in one human family, be able to transcend nationalism, tribalism, and ideological differences and move toward a sense of belonging to humanity as a whole.

To contribute to the development of this consciousness, progressive and peace-loving groups must participate with deliberate, intentional activities in society. Also, a broad and serious discussion on the application of scientific technology must take place in society. The process of engaging in this debate is itself an educational process and will result in elevating the collective social consciousness.

Ikeda: I am in complete agreement with your point about the necessity for a broad-based discussion. It is essential that we strengthen efforts in this direction.

I myself am deeply concerned about the division and conflict in contemporary society. I am acutely aware of the need, even more so today, for harmony and understanding based on a thorough dialogue on the issues. Though opinions may differ, people surely can find common ground on the issues of world peace and the coexistence of humankind.

Chapter 9

Loyalty to Humanity: Competition with a Human Face

Ikeda: Professor Rotblat, I recall that in October 2001 you came all the way from London to visit the newly opened Soka University of America (SUA) campus in Orange County, California.

It was shortly after the terrorist attacks on the US on September 11 and at the height of the panic when many people were canceling their visits to the US. Despite the fearful mood in the country, you came all the way to California to visit. You left a glorious and ever-lasting page in SUA history. As the founder of Soka University of America, I appreciate your sincerity and would like to once again thank you from the bottom of my heart.

Rotblat: Yes. I remember the time well. I never would have thought of canceling my trip. On the contrary, the situation made me want to visit SUA all the more. When I arrived at Los Angeles airport, I had a sore throat and had no voice, so the SUA people asked me if I wanted to cancel my talk the following day. I replied, "I'm sure that I will be better tomorrow." And so I gave my talk as scheduled. Once I commit to an engagement, I do not casually cancel it.

I am not a practitioner of Buddhism, but, Dr. Ikeda, you and I work toward the same goals and have the same beliefs, and I feel that we have a strong friendship. As we talk, I know that we are on the same wavelength. This is why I was very happy to get together to talk with the people at SUA whose very important mission I endorse completely.

Ikeda: The students at SUA were very impressed, Professor Rotblat, with the way that you spoke up with all your might, in spite of your health challenges.

On hearing you speak on the topic, "The Quest for Global Peace", one student commented, "We are not seeking a passive peace that is merely an absence of war. We want to usher in an era of true peace in which everyone is happy. Everyone felt inspired to commit themselves to nurture the desire to contribute to humanity and become persons who shine a bright light in each of our chosen professions."

The students, who graduated this May [2005], have entered a new phase of their lives in high spirits.

Rotblat: Admirable. I am truly excited and happy for them. I was deeply impressed by the students' response to my talk. After I spoke, a number of students came up to meet me. I was very encouraged by talking with these young people, and it even made me feel youthful and energized myself. I looked forward to their graduation.

Please tell the students at SUA to remember what I mentioned in my talk; that is, I hope that they will spend their wonderful youth contributing to society.

These are the young people who will carry on after our generation. I wanted to confirm that they will take seriously their responsibility for the future. I wanted to tell them that they must take responsibility for their actions and always be able to say, from the bottom of their hearts, that they are working for the benefit of humanity.

Ikeda: Thank you for that message. We have no choice but to entrust the future to the youth of today. I agree with you completely and also do my best to nurture and encourage young people. People are our most precious resource.

The founding goal of Soka University of America is to foster a steady stream of global citizens. Professor Rotblat, in your talk at SUA, you emphasized the importance of cultivating a sense of loyalty to the whole of humankind.

Rotblat: Yes. When I refer to "global citizens", I am not thinking of an official status signifying citizenship in a global nation-state or a centralized government whose people hold international passports or other trappings of this identity. The time may come for such things, but first of all, some form of global governance will evolve, and people will have a sense of something beyond their interdependent relationship with their own nation-state.

To prepare for this next stage, we must tackle certain tasks, including educating ourselves to heighten our own sense of belonging to a global community.

In one sense, this "loyalty to the whole of humankind" includes a utilitarian aspect. In other words, it is linked to our ultimate goal of ensuring the survival of the human race. From this perspective, we can see clearly that this is a natural extension of other forms of loyalty.

5. Professor Joseph Rotblat lectures at Soka University of America, 2001.

From national interest to the benefit of humankind

Ikeda: At every opportunity, I have urged that we make the conceptual transition from pursuing national interests to working for the benefit of humankind. The key to this process is offering a global education that furthers the acceptance and understanding of diverse values and cultures. It is essential that, with open hearts and minds, we engage with people in a way that helps cultivate a global perspective and sense of understanding and empathy toward others who are different from ourselves.

Educational contexts that instill a global perspective and nurture this kind of global citizenship will become even more important during this century. My motive for founding Soka University of America was based on this conviction.

Rotblat: Education is extremely important. Our various loyalties can be viewed in terms of a series of concentric circles centered on the self. The smallest circle to which people have a sense of loyalty represents the family, and next is one's neighborhood. The outermost and largest circle, in the consciousness of people today, represents the nation-state. I strongly advocate that one larger concentric circle be added, that is, a circle representing loyalty to and a sense of identity with all of humankind.

Ikeda: This is a profound concept that resonates with Buddhist teachings. In Buddhism, the small self that is consumed with ego is called *"shôga"*. The larger, more mature and developed self that takes on the suffering of all creation as its own is called *"taiga"*. It is the sense of merging with the timeless and spatially infinite universal life force.

"The human revolution" is what we call the dynamic expansion of one's reality in the transition from the smaller to the larger self, and ultimately, this dynamism is the force behind the creation of movements for social change. Humanity has advanced into space. From the cosmic viewpoint, global unification is the current of this age. We should not be prepossessed with the small circle enclosing the self.

Compassion in an integrated globe

Rotblat: In contemporary society, the integration of the entire globe is progressing rapidly due to the development of communications and transportation. The advances of science and technology are linking people together. In previous times, people in differing regions were unable to communicate with each other. When I was born, the telephone and telegraph had just been introduced. Before that, if a person wanted to send a message, it was sent by boat on a long voyage.

People living on different islands were cut off from each other and had no means of communication. Consequently, many independent nation-states developed in their own worlds. Each was isolated from the other. This all changed after marvelous progress was made in telecommunications and information exchange. Now, anyone can find out about anything happening anywhere in the world almost instantaneously. For example, if an earthquake hits Japan, one can find out about it almost immediately.

Ikeda: In October of last year, a major earthquake struck the Chuetsu region of Niigata Prefecture. At that time, you kindly sent us a warm letter of sympathy, for which I express SGI's gratitude again.

The news of the disaster raced around the world and people were able to share the suffering with the victims. I prayed earnestly that the souls of the deceased would rest in peace and that the area would recover from the disaster as soon as possible.

The development of communications technology is one factor that has made the world seem smaller and more closely integrated. The problem is how to make this factor contribute in a positive way to the happiness of humanity and social evolution.

A fearless optimism

Rotblat: Unfortunately, this same science and technology has produced the means for people to kill each other with greater facility. We have now acquired the power to destroy each other completely. This is another side of the development of science and technology.

The issue is which side will win in this competition. Will we join forces for good, or will we destroy each other? We must learn how to coexist together; otherwise we will surely end up killing each other off.

Ikeda: Recently, I have become aware that people around the world have begun to feel more sympathy for other people in distant regions who are suffering from poverty, starvation. Empathy, and the feeling that others' pain is our pain, seems evident. If this trend accelerates, the times will certainly change. Indeed, they must.

Rotblat: We have indeed become closer to one another. When I talk about the world as a global village, this is, of course, a symbolic reference to a rural village society. It points to the very real human relationships in a village, and the importance of knowing and being known by everyone. Now, with the help of advances in science and technology, we can become global citizens, just as if we were residents of one village. When disaster strikes, we can know exactly what has occurred, and so are able to help each other more. This is one positive result of scientific and technological development.

Ikeda: In his early twentieth-century work entitled *A Geography of Human Life*, Tsunesaburo Makiguchi, the first president of Soka Gakkai, expressed the insight that humankind must turn from military, political, and economic competition to a humanitarian kind of competition. He predicted that a transition to a humanitarian paradigm would ultimately become the trend of the times.

Professor Rotblat, how do you view the future of humankind? Do you have an optimistic or pessimistic perspective of the future?

Rotblat: I feel that I must be an optimist. What is the alternative? If we all succumb to pessimism, we will only destroy each other. The only sensible option is to be optimistic. Yet, it takes effort to be an optimist. I cannot be optimistic naturally. When I say I am an optimist, I do not simply believe that world conditions will improve of their own accord. Nothing will change unless we make an effort to make the world a better place. Each person must do whatever he or she can to contribute something to this effort.

Ikeda: Yes. An optimist must have a grounded philosophy and firm convictions. A true optimist is one who understands the harsh realities, yet has the resolute will to overcome any obstacle and trusts in the unlimited potential of the human spirit. Finally, actions must substantiate these firm convictions.

Nichiren Buddhism, of which I am a practitioner, pulses with this fearless optimism. Nichiren, who lived in Japan during the thirteenth century, endured numerous episodes of repression and persecution. He admonished his disciples "to be prepared for the worst, and not to expect good times, but take the bad times for granted."[1] He further said that "you should understand that, when one practices the Lotus Sutra under such circumstances, difficulties will arise, and these are to be looked on as 'peaceful' practices."[2] Also, he reassured them that "winter always turns to spring."[3] In the midst of adversity, Nichiren expounded Buddhism and took actions to ensure the happiness of the people.

Above all, a courageous optimism provides the strength to overcome all obstacles and bring about change. A pessimistic view cannot produce any creative energy.

Rotblat: Yes, that's true. Optimism is the ethic I live by. It is not a religious sentiment, but it may be similar to your religious views. Dr. Ikeda, we start off from different points, but we arrive at the same conclusions.

"Read for personal growth, learn for the sake of virtue"

Ikeda: The Buddhist scriptures (*The Dharma Analysis Treasury*, or *Kusharon* in Japanese) teach that hope has the power to nurture the body and extend one's life span. Professor Rotblat, your long and hope-filled life dedicated to peace is evidence of what boundless optimism can do. Please share your wisdom with the youth of today. What kind of advice can you give them? For example, how do you view the importance of becoming familiar with great literature and the rich spiritual legacy of humankind?

Rotblat: One of the characteristics of the new century is that knowledge in many fields such as science, culture, ethics, and society, while still primarily obtained from books and other publications, has become accessible from a variety of sources such as the Internet, television, and radio. However, books are still the most fundamental forum for the expression of one's views and thoughts. In any case, if one hopes to make a contribution to society, I would advise the young to study the views of great people.

Ikeda: I have heard that when you were young, you loved to read Rabindranath Tagore, Jack London, Jules Verne, and Romain Rolland.

Rotblat: That's right. They represent different genres, but I loved them all during my childhood. Tagore is an Indian poet, Jack London an adventure novelist, and Jules Verne a science-fiction writer. Each of the books I read added to my store of knowledge and helped clarify my sense of mission. They assisted in the formation of my value orientation and view of life.

One caution regarding reading is that some books have been written by fanatical authors, or they were written for the express purpose of making money. Meaningless and trashy content is being published, so we must be very discriminating in our choice of reading material.

Ikeda: That is right. At every opportunity, I emphasize to young people the importance of reading good books. When I was young, I studied under Mr. Josei Toda, Soka Gakkai's second president, who sternly urged me every day to read good books. He would scold me furiously if he saw me reading one of the coarse and tasteless weekly magazines. He would tell me, "Human beings should live to create and enjoy a cultured life, read for personal growth and development, and learn for the sake of virtue". Even now, I recall vividly his sharp admonition, "If you poison your mind with these entertaining pieces of fiction, written for sale, then you are sabotaging your life and losing all sense of direction."

In the younger years especially, it is important to expand one's horizons by reading widely across a broad range of disciplines. Professor Rotblat, what kind of works do you recommend in the field of science?

Read to know our world

Rotblat: Since we live in an age of science, I believe that everyone should have at least a certain degree of scientific knowledge. Therefore, for instance, it is important to read about the nature of space and books related to science.

The English theoretical physicist Stephen W. Hawking is a great scientist, who, despite paralysis and the loss of almost all his ability to convey information, including the function of speech, overcame his physical limitations and wrote several important works, one of which is *A Brief History of Time*.[4] This is not an easy book to read, because it is packed with information. But if you can make it to the end, you will have a good understanding of what he is saying. I have heard that recently, simplified versions of his books have been published.

Ikeda: The Japanese editions of Professor Hawking's popular works such as *The Universe in a Nutshell*[5] and *A Brief History of Time* became bestsellers in Japan. Hawking continued his research in spite of battling amyotrophic lateral sclerosis, an incurable disease. The example of Hawking's life, in which he lectures and writes by means of a portable computer and voice synthesizer, testifies to the unlimited human potential in each of us.

Rotblat: Yes. Another author I appreciate very much is Martin Rees, who condenses the major scientific and technological achievements of the previous century and explores the meaning they have for humankind. He was granted the title of Astronomer Royal in the UK, and is an important figure in the world of science. I recommend his books highly.[6]

It is also important to read about history. For example, Richard Rhodes published two volumes on the process leading to the invention of the nuclear bomb.[7] The first volume discusses how the nuclear bomb was created, and the second describes the development of the hydrogen bomb.

I could cite many other science-related works for the general public. If people read these books, they will gain a better understanding of what is happening in the world and be able to make their own judgments.

In a democratic country, people are supposed to be able to choose their leaders, which means that they play a role in choosing their national legislators and president. How can we avoid being confused by campaign propaganda, and how can we make accurate judgments? Knowing the facts is the most important factor. If one reads well-researched and accurate books, then the facts will be clear. And by so doing, one can make one's own decisions and not be at the mercy of media journalism.

Ikeda: Today, people are overwhelmed with the sheer volume of information, and clear sight and engagement of the heart are needed for them to separate right from wrong. To develop a discerning eye for the truth requires cultivating intellect. Also, one must develop one's mind and develop an accurate sense of history. This is what I constantly urge young people to do.

Incidentally, what do you think about poetry? I have heard that you read the revered poet Rabindranath Tagore when you were a youth.

Rotblat: That was such a long time ago. Dr. Ikeda, you have written some superb poetry as well.

Ikeda: Thank you very much. I want to offer my deepest appreciation for the wonderful introduction you wrote for the English edition of my poetry collection, *Fighting for Peace*.

Rotblat: Your poetry is beautiful and is filled with a message of hope and reflections on fear, and dreams. You express yourself in a way that immediately resonates in my heart. This is why I love reading the refined work of contemporary poets such as you, Dr. Ikeda.

I sincerely believe that, as I wrote in my introduction, your poetry "offers hope to those in despair, strengthens the weak, and gives courage to those who have been defeated."[8]

Ikeda: Thank you for those kind words. My work aside, generally speaking, I believe that poetry has the infinite power to enrich and expand the mind. Poetry transcends national boundaries and great distances, and is able to link hearts and minds together, in the same way that music does. Discrimination is non-existent in the world of poetry. This is why I treasure poetry.

Professor Rotblat, I have heard that you have written poetry that addresses the topic of peace.

Rotblat: Yes, but it appears that I have not been blessed by the muse of poetry. I like the study of language. I study the source and meaning of words, and am interested in learning new words. I write in prose to express myself.

High hopes for the next generation

Ikeda: Poetry is not simply a literary form. It can be described as the passion to inspire. Your poetry as well as other works are infused with thoughts of peace, and I hope that they will come to be read widely.

Thus far, we have discussed the legacy we want to share with humankind. Finally, I would like to ask about your hopes and expectations for young people.

The Pugwash Conferences hold high hopes for the Student/Young Pugwash Group. What were the circumstances for founding this group for young scientists?

Rotblat: As we discussed previously, the Pugwash Conferences organization was founded to give leading scientists the opportunity to coordinate their efforts. Similarly, the Russell–Einstein Manifesto was signed and supported by scientists who were of the same mind.

We must also think about the future. I am probably the oldest, but we older people tend to talk to others who are just as old as us. We have many areas of understanding and agreement among ourselves, but we must devote all our efforts to nurture the up-and-coming generation so that they can survive and build a world that is much better than the one we are leaving them. We must ensure that the tragedies of history are never repeated.

Accordingly, the Pugwash Conferences have always included and nurtured the younger generation of scientists, especially at the university level. We believe that the issues debated at the Pugwash Conferences should be part of the intellectual discourse in the educational arena. To make sure that younger scientists are exposed to these ideas, we formed the Student/Young Pugwash Group.

Ikeda: You had great foresight. You remind me of the encounters I have had with former South African President Nelson Mandela. I asked him whether he had groomed a successor to follow him. I wanted to say that if he had no youthful successor, then his 10,000-day prison term, served during the days of his human rights struggle, would have been all for naught. Smiling, the former president answered, "Yes. I do have a successor."

In Soka Gakkai International, our movement for peace and cultural enrichment has placed great importance on, and devoted considerable energy to, nurturing the youth. Our second president, Josei Toda, who established the foundation of today's movement, often stressed, "A new era will be built by the passion and energy of youth."

It is interesting that the Student/Young Pugwash members are so much younger than you, so I would also like to know how you feel about interacting with them?

To liaise with youth

Rotblat: I am the oldest member of the Pugwash Conferences, but age doesn't make any difference. I have very good relationships with the younger members. When I was younger, I didn't think that I could relate to someone much older or younger than I was. However, now, my assistant is sixty years younger than me, but I have never been concerned about the age difference between us. We are like brothers, encouraging each other and working together as colleagues.

Ikeda: That's marvelous. You are able to relate so well probably because you are always humble and young at heart.

Rotblat: Actually, I have never thought of myself as an old person. I always feel like I am a young person. The only exception is that the human body has limitations, and these days, I have felt the effects of aging in my physical body. But this is only in my body, because my spirit is still the same. I still feel like my youthful self.

In spite of the fact that I am the oldest member of the Pugwash Conferences, I was appointed as the liaison between the youth group and the older members. I am happy to say that both groups relate to each other very well.

Ikeda: It was our first president Tsunesaburo Makiguchi's habit to often say, in his seventies, "We, the youth!" in a spirited, rousing voice. Professor Rotblat, you are a model of lifelong youth.

Rotblat: I visited Seoul in October of last year [2004] and had a very pleasant experience. All the members of the Student/Young Pugwash

Group were there. They were all former students of mine. They said that they wanted to use my name for their next project. I was very honored. I was very happy when it was announced at the Seoul conference.

Ikeda: I understand why they wanted to recognize and honor you, their teacher. The teacher–student relationship is one of the most noble of human relationships. I also express my appreciation and honor my own mentor as I introduce his legacy to the world.

Rotblat: The passion of youth is so precious. As people age, it invariably seems that various factors wear on them and completely tire them out. The passion, energy, and enthusiasm of youth sometimes become excessive and too extreme. Yet, even so, they are important. I always make an effort to be gentle and avoid crushing or discouraging a young person's enthusiasm. I also try to cheer them on so that their passion can continue burning brightly.

Ikeda: That's because you are a model leader. There is no other way to build a peaceful global society than to nurture many young people and to encourage them to devote themselves to working for the benefit and happiness of humanity.

I pledge, with renewed determination, and with our common vision in my heart, to advance peace education and education for global citizenship, so that we may build a hopeful future for humankind.

CHAPTER 10

Toward a World Without War: The United Nations and We the People

Ikeda: Some people say that human history is a history of war and violence. This may be true, but at the same time, one could also say that it is a history of assiduous efforts and challenges to eliminate the horrors of war. Throughout the war-and-violence-ravaged twentieth century, a system was created based on a consensus that called for a shift away from an ethos of "might makes right" to the "rule of law", thanks especially to the sacrifices and heroic efforts of many who brought justice to international society. The United Nations, needless to say, has been central to this effort.

Today, however, both the rule of law as well as the United Nations itself are facing serious crises. UN secretary-general Kofi Annan issued a stern warning in his speech at the 2004 UN General Assembly. Referring to the need to restore respect for the rule of law, he said, "To do so, we must start with the principle that no one is above the law, no one should be denied its protection. Every nation that proclaims the rule of law at home must respect it abroad, and every nation that insists on it abroad must enforce it at home."[1]

In the same speech, the secretary-general called for a reformation of the United Nations—a bulwark for the rule of law, founded in the ashes of World War II, a war that brought untold sorrow to humankind.

Personally, I am extremely alarmed about the continued efforts, even into the twenty-first century, to legitimize the philosophy of "might makes right" rather than the rule of law.

Seeking legitimacy in a multi-cultural world

Rotblat: To create a world without war, a system of global governance is necessary. The first step toward this goal is the reinvigoration of the United Nations. This is why I have been a supporter of the UN from the very beginning.

The United Nations now has 191 member countries. Of course, each country has its own economic conditions, cultural traditions, and various perspectives on the issues. For everyone to come together on all issues is a time-consuming as well as complicated process. This is why people say that the UN is powerless and complain that it takes so long to reach conclusions. However, this is the only way to solve problems in a democratic manner.

Ikeda: Certainly, the democratic system has many problems and is not completely flawless. However, it is a fact that no other better system exists. As Winston Churchill once said, "Democracy is the worst form of government except for all those other forms that have been tried from time to time."[2] The same can be said of the United Nations, the organization that embodies democracy in the international political sphere.

The United Nations may appear to be an inefficient, powerless, and deplorable organization at times. Still, the UN functions, and the world is far better off with the UN than without it. President John F. Kennedy said in his 1961 UN speech, "The problem is not the death of one man; the problem is the life of this organization. It will either grow to meet the challenges of our age, or it will be gone with the wind, without influence, without force, without respect. Were we to let it die, to enfeeble its power, to cripple its powers, we would condemn our future."[3] That speech carries a message increasingly relevant for today's world.

Rotblat: Would we choose to live under a despotic regime in which we would not be permitted to voice our own opinions, and all affairs would be swiftly dispatched? Or would we choose to reach agreements satisfactory to all, no matter how much time and effort it takes?

If we wish to take the latter option, the path of democracy, then, we must provide the opportunity for diverse people and groups to express their opinions. This is why the role of non-governmental organizations [NGOs] is becoming even more important.

Ikeda: These days we must make the difficult decision about how to support the framework of UN-centered multilateralism.

The discord created in the international community by the Iraq War shows us that if we do not seek the basis for legitimacy in the multilateral framework, then the international social order does not function well. In this sense, the cries claiming that the United Nations is facing a crisis could be reframed in terms that recognize the opportunity for the United Nations to reassert itself in the international sphere. Accordingly, rather than view the process of reforming the United Nations in narrow terms, we must see it as an opportunity truly to activate, strengthen, and make substantial improvements.

And as you say, Professor Rotblat, this process must promote democratic decision making in the organization. In this regard, one issue that must be addressed is respect for democratic principles in the relationships between nations. This includes the issue of the composition of the permanent members on the UN Security Council. In the future, abolition of the veto power should be seriously reviewed.

Democratic participation in the UN will also be enhanced by allowing the wishes of the people to be reflected in the decision-making process through the inclusion of NGOs. This is a suggestion that I have made every year in my New Year's address on SGI Day [January 26]. I have proposed a reform plan directly to each successive secretary-general. For example, in addition to the present UN General Assembly, which includes the representatives of the current member countries, I suggest a People's General Assembly that would include NGOs and the companies, labor unions, and other citizens' groups participating in the UN Global Compact. This would modify the present system into a bi-cameral [two-chamber] system.

In March of this year [2005], UN secretary-general Kofi Annan announced in his report on UN reform that mechanisms for engaging fully and systematically with civil society must be established. I would hope to see a bold resolution and sustained efforts to achieve this goal. In addition, to address the UN's chronic funding deficit, I think that as well as the current allotted share of funding from member countries, it would also be good to solicit funds widely from private sources. I also proposed this point to Mr. Boutros Boutros-Ghali, the former secretary-general, when I met with him in Tokyo in 1993.

A role for civil society

Rotblat: I believe that people have the power to influence society. No effort is a waste. When a small stone is thrown into a pond, the ripples travel widely out from the center. Though the ripples may become less powerful, they still do not disappear completely. Every person has the power to create ripples that can change society. If these efforts are concentrated and channeled through NGOs, inevitably the power to influence society will grow.

Ikeda: With the advance of globalization, the problems that the UN deals with, such as security issues, human rights, environmental problems, development, and cultural diversity, have become difficult to address satisfactorily only in negotiations and agreements between individual countries. In response to the impact of globalization, we must change the way we govern and manage the various systems on the entire earth. When we do, as you pointed out, Professor Rotblat, the role of the civil sector will only increase.

Actually, now, the civil sector does more than simply collaborate with the UN; it is one of the main supports for the UN. Also, as we saw in the creation of the Treaty to Ban Land Mines through a solidarity of more than one thousand non-governmental organizations around the world, and in the World Court Project that won recognition of the illegality of nuclear weapons at the International Court of Justice, civil society truly is a force that impacts international politics.

Rotblat: Solidarity is so important. If we unite, we can change the world. It might take some time, but viewed from a long-term perspective, the people will be victorious in the end. Of course, we will have to wait much longer before ideals based on the human conscience become the main definitive standard for governmental policies. However, already, many volunteer groups and NGOs have adopted this standard as they pursue their specific goal-directed activities.

Among these are groups with a long history such as the International Committee of the Red Cross, but many have been formed in recent years. These include, for example, Amnesty International, Oxfam [Oxford Famine Relief Committee], Greenpeace, Physicians for Social Responsibility, and of course, the Pugwash Conferences.

These groups are global social movements and have made substantial contributions to expanding the meaning of citizenship and nurturing a sense of loyalty to humankind.

Ikeda: Yes. It has been reported that in 1914, there were 1,083 NGOs, but in the year 2000, 37,000 NGOs were in existence. The spread of solidarity between people that transcends national boundaries first grew in response to the impact of transnational environmental problems. But now, a huge groundswell of activity continues to build as people question, and seek to limit, the influence of nation-centered governance and to establish alternative institutions.

As I view these circumstances, I recall Arnold Toynbee's great work, *A Study of History*.[4] Professor Toynbee contended that when ruling countries become central to a civilization, this does not mark the zenith of a civilization, but the process of its decline and collapse. In other words, in the decline of a civilization, internal fractures spread, political leaders scheme to maintain their supremacy through might, and a "universal state" emerges. However, this "universal state" enters into its death throes as it is assaulted by an external proletariat, which strikes with physical, violent opposition from the outside and by an internal proletariat, from which emerges a spiritual and nonviolent resistance from inside the state.

From within this internal proletariat comes the spiritual foundation for the next civilization. Here, I am not tempted to refer to any particular country today as the "universal state". I am not expecting a catastrophe either. Rather, since the leaders of the world are unable to deal effectively with the numerous problems threatening to destroy the international community such as nuclear weapons, environmental devastation, and wrenching poverty, I think it is especially important that global citizens, united in solidarity beyond national borders, will embrace the spiritual values of nonviolence and mutual coexistence, and will change the current of public opinion.

I believe that we, the members of SGI, who make up a united force of citizens from 190 countries and regions, have a responsibility in this process, and I think that Professor Toynbee would agree, especially since he predicted that the spiritual basis for the new civilization would arise in East Asia, which would initiate the current towards peace.

A new paradigm regarding security

Rotblat: As you say, to win universal support for the idea of a world without war, there must be a new mental paradigm regarding security issues. Today, at a time when military conflict threatens the very survival of humankind itself, we must think seriously of ways to eliminate this threat.

In the distant past, the security of family was the major concern of human beings. Next, people became concerned with securing the safety of their country. Today, we must consciously begin to think in terms of the security of all of humankind. Throughout the flow of history, human beings have gradually shifted the focus of their loyalty to larger and larger groups. Now, we must take the final step to cultivate a sense of loyalty to all of humanity. The problem is that the concept of humanity tends to be vague and abstract in people's minds. Certainly, it is difficult to elicit a warm, intimate feeling toward a group composed of 6.5 billion people. However, if we limit this to the issue of loyalty, the size of the group should not be a problem.

To prove this point, consider the United States, a country of 260 million people who possess extremely diverse racial and ethnic characteristics. The citizens of the US have a much stronger sense of belonging to their country than do citizens of other nations ten times smaller. More important than size is the sense of shared values, the ability to participate actively in political affairs, and a shared concern about the economic, social, and cultural issues confronting the nation. Given these factors, we are hopeful that the potential for nurturing a sense of loyalty toward all humankind will unfold over time.

Ikeda: About 100 years ago, the first president of Soka Gakkai, Mr. Tsunesaburo Makiguchi, made the following statement. He said that all human beings should possess three types of awareness: they should be aware of themselves first as community residents who possess deeply rooted ties to their local communities, second, as citizens of their country, and third, as global citizens whose lives are intimately related to the entire world. In other words, with a firm sense of belonging to and understanding of both the local community as well as the global community, people will be free of the narrow-minded tendencies of nationalism and ethnicity.

During Makiguchi's time, though Japan became increasingly fascist, Makiguchi stayed true to his beliefs. As a result of his firm convictions, the authorities viewed him as a threat and sent him to prison, where he died.

Nationalism is a philosophy that is artificially formed under special conditions during certain periods. On the other hand, patriotism is a natural sentiment that transcends the conditions of any given historical period and is not limited to the framework of the nation-state.

I have had the opportunity to meet a number of astronauts and cosmonauts, and they all say that when they view the earth from the vast expanse of space, they feel a powerful sense of sentimental attachment and sense of themselves as citizens of the earth. They speak and act from a desire to contribute to the common good of all humankind.

Professor Rotblat, I share your idea that reinforcement of a sense of global citizenship is essential.

Rotblat: One of the greatest difficulties to overcome in the process of creating global citizens is dealing with the conflicts between people who identify strongly with their respective countries. The nation-state, which has developed over the past several centuries, is characterized by a national identity and people's protectiveness of this identity. In other words, the nation-state is based on the concept of national sovereignty and a tendency to emphasize differences with other nation-states.

Further, the major function of the nation-state is said to be to protect its people from the threats of other nation-states. This has been understood to mean that nations have the right to maintain war-making potential. Anatol Rapoport, a leading political scientist of international affairs, addresses this issue. He writes,

> It is regarded as axiomatic that the autonomy of a state is secured by its sovereignty, and sovereignty by its war potential. Thus a war establishment is universally held to be an indispensable institution in practically every state … . The survival prospects of the institution of war, on the one hand, and of the nation-state as we know it, on the other, are closely related.[5]

Indeed, to eliminate the "institution of war", we must overcome the thorny problem of national sovereignty.

Ikeda: As you say, the "institution of war" is related to the issue of national sovereignty. However, considering that most of the conflicts after the Cold War were not between countries with established war potential but were domestic conflicts, it must be noted that eliminating warfare in any form is not simply a matter of dismantling the nation-state system. On the contrary, if the monopoly that nations have on weapons of violence is

relinquished for a state of anarchy, and a power vacuum develops, then violence may very well spread everywhere.

Therefore, the focus is not on eliminating the nation-state, but rather on
how to regulate and manage the clear over-extension of national sovereignty in which countries possess weapons powerful enough to extinguish
the entire human race.

6. Professor Arnold Toynbee and Dr. Daisaku Ikeda in London, 1972.

Establishing international mechanisms to ensure peace

Rotblat: In the near future, this concept of sovereignty will mutate under
the influence of the idea of autonomy. In Rapoport's terms, autonomy is
"the independence within a certain policy environment that is limited by a
sense of responsibility to a high level of organization."

The most important element of national sovereignty, which is the right
and capability to wage war, must be eliminated. No country would be permitted to begin a war. Rephrased, a standing military is unnecessary.

In other words, this would mean the extinction of a national military and
the recognition of a police force under the jurisdiction of some kind of global organization, which has a prescribed enforcement capacity to maintain
the peace. No country would be permitted to declare war against another.

This will be difficult for people to accept, because we are still bound by the concept of the nation-state.

However, by promoting the cooperative aspects of national autonomy and inhibiting divisive tendencies, the nation-state would survive as a link between the individual and a stable and peaceful international community.

Ikeda: Lord Bertrand Russell and Professor Albert Einstein, the central signatories of the Russell–Einstein Manifesto, advocated the idea that military power be concentrated under the jurisdiction of a world government. Mahatma Gandhi also advanced this idea.

In the past, Norman Cousins and I discussed in great detail the directions that the United Nations reforms might take. Mr. Cousins raised the idea that a federation of states would be the most appropriate form for the UN. He felt that the jurisdiction of a world federation would be clearly delineated and maintained based on the shared sovereignty within the federation and the sovereignty maintained by the nation-states. The value of pursuing this course will certainly be examined more fully in the future.

Rotblat: Einstein was a great scientist, and he was also quite knowledgeable about politics. He concluded that we must discover some form of world governance to save humanity. By this, he did not mean that we would all pay allegiance to the same despotic ruler. The nation-state would probably remain intact and maintain its own characteristic autonomy. Its cultural functions of supporting the development of language and literature would be especially important to preserve.

In his 1947 letter entitled "To the General Assembly of the United Nations", Einstein wrote, "The United Nations is an extremely important and useful institution provided the peoples and Governments of the world realize that it is merely a transitional system toward a final goal, which is the establishment of a supranational authority vested with sufficient legislative and executive power to keep the peace."

Bertrand Russell felt that a world government was the only option that would prevent humankind from destroying itself. In his 1961 publication *Has Man a Future?*, Russell emphasized the necessity for a world government and explored the structure of such an entity. He wrote, "These technical advances, while they have made present international anarchy infinitely more dangerous than it used to be, have also made it technically possible to establish a World Government which would be able to exert its power everywhere and could make armed resistance virtually impossible."[6]

Ikeda: Both men advocated a world government entity that has yet to materialize. However, the idea of "global governance" that evolved from their work has been embraced by various actors central to the United Nations, including nations, NGOs, corporations, and individuals who have agreed to try to create a multi-dimensional earth government.

The major issue of global politics that I believe must be tackled is how to create an international system of global governance. Even without a world government, we see in the trend toward regionally based governmental structures such as the European Union, a shift from a national sovereignty-based governmental form. In other words, we are witnessing the process of an experiment in human history. Perhaps the transfer of sovereignty from the nation-state will proceed first of all, not at the international level, but within separate regions. In Asia, there is the conceptual framework of an East Asian regional community.

In order to accelerate this process, in my Peace Proposal, which I delivered at the beginning of this year [2005], I proposed the establishment of an Asian United Nations Headquarters.

Rotblat: During the Cold War, actualizing the concept of a world government was completely unrealistic. However, today those great ideological struggles have been put to rest, and the greatest obstacle to establishing a world government has been removed.

Today, the time is ripe for a serious examination of the conditions necessary for establishing international mechanisms to ensure a lasting world peace. Of course, the bold attempt to actually build such a system will not succeed without a lengthy and dedicated effort. Opposition would undoubtedly come from special interests that have benefited from inciting conflict between nations. Also, even those who would never condone conflict might put up stiff resistance to efforts to establish international mechanisms, primarily because of their desire to protect the sovereignty of their own nations.

Furthermore, some express concern that the administrators of the world government may not be moderate and unbiased, and others fear that a gargantuan bureaucracy will develop. These are all reasonable concerns. Accordingly, it appears that a world government may have to wait until sometime in the future. Yet, it will still be a vision we hold in our minds continually.

The kind of world government that I proposed may seem unrealistic now, but eventually its manifestation will seem more possible. I will look forward to that time.

Toward peace based on law

Ikeda: I feel the same way. We must seek to abolish standing armies and establish a federation of free countries. This desire, needless to say, originated with Kant's "Perpetual Peace", written more than 200 years ago. Kant's ideal of a federation of nations is given expression today in the United Nations, and in the policies having to do with abolition of standing armies, such as Article Nine of the Japanese constitution and the actual abolition of the armed forces of Costa Rica.

Kant's philosophy of peace aimed to be a peace based on law. He contended, not that law would determine whether war was right or wrong, but that war was fundamentally wrong, and that we must create a system in which war could not occur. According to Kant, the proposition that nations should not go to war should take priority in any discussion on the subject.

The fact, however, that a major war broke out during efforts to make war illegal, namely during the Hague Peace Conference and the Paris Convention, ultimately means that we cannot prevent war just by treaties or systems unless there exists a strong will on the part of the people. After World War II, the United Nations was established thanks to people's remorse and awareness that another war would imperil human survival, and their detemination to never again allow another such war to take place.

Whether we can abolish war depends on our ability to create a system where all the human wisdom can be gathered, although the creation of such a system seems cumbersome.

If war is ever to be abolished, ultimately it will be done by nurturing a "fortress of peace" in people's hearts, and by cultivating the will to live in peace through education, in the broadest sense of the word.

Rotblat: I believe this, too. Abolition of the institution of war will be based on the assumption that a radical shift in our view of the nation is made. This will require the establishment of an educational process that nurtures in the hearts of individuals a sense of loyalty toward all of humankind.

As in the case of all educational processes, the realization of this objective will take a lengthy period of time. However, first of all, most important is that we begin the process. As a fitting point of departure, I would like to reiterate this motto: "If you want peace, prepare for peace." In Latin, "*Si vis pacem, para pacem.*" I believe that within this mind-set is the conviction that there is a way to protect humanity, our most precious common resource. We must convince our political leaders that the only way to achieve peace is to "prepare for peace". It is critically important that we create a culture of peace.

Ikeda: Dr. Elise Boulding offered a wonderful definition of "culture of peace" in a dialogue we shared. She defined it as a culture in which people "deal creatively with their differences and share their resources". The question is how we interact with others. If people do not accept those who are different from themselves, a monochromatic world results, and confrontations continue between different cultures and civilizations.

Despite claiming that we respect others or that we are tolerant of others, if we continue to take an absolutist view, insisting that our own culture and civilization are superior, then the world will stay divided. The key to avoid succumbing to these tendencies, as Dr. Boulding says, is to share and, through dialogue, seek to change ourselves as well as others in the process.

We SGI members believe our mission is to seek and disseminate widely the way to transform ourselves and others through dialogue.

Thank you, Professor Rotblat, for devoting your precious time and energy to this dialogue series conducted over such a long period of time. I am deeply grateful to you for sincerely and passionately sharing with us your philosophy of hope and perspectives on humanity's future in our mutual quest for global peace. Your contributions have made this a significant dialogue.

Rotblat: Likewise, I am truly thrilled that you made it possible to realize my long-held wish to engage in a dialogue with you, Dr. Ikeda. I offer you my best wishes for your continued and ever more active participation in endeavors to create a world without war and nuclear weapons.

APPENDIX 1

Declaration Against Nuclear Weapons
by Josei Toda, second president of Soka Gakkai

The declaration published here was announced by Soka Gakkai's second president Josei Toda on September 8, 1957, at Mitsuzawa Stadium in Yokohama. Mr. Toda used the occasion of a Soka Gakkai young men's division sports festival to make it public, but what gave rise to the thoughts in the declaration was his two-year incarceration during World War II, when, together with first president Tsunesaburo Makiguchi, he was imprisoned by Japan's military government for what were then considered subversive thoughts: opposing war. At the time he chose to announce his declaration, Mr. Toda was troubled by the thought that his time was limited as his own life was nearing its close. He chose to leave this declaration as his final will to the youth division members and, through them, to the world.

A word of explanation is in order concerning his use of the word literally translated in the declaration as "devil". In speaking from the Buddhist point of view, "devil" refers to those tendencies existing within human life itself that, when set in motion, sap people's life force and torment the human heart and mind. The epitome of this destructive function is, in Mr. Toda's thinking, nuclear weapons. When Mr. Toda called for execution of anyone using nuclear weapons, he was not thinking in terms of legislating an actual death penalty. He chose those words as the clearest way to vilify the devilish function within human nature that attempts to justify the use of nuclear weapons.

At the opposite pole from the devilish functions existing in human life is a life brimming with compassion and creative force. If the one may be called the functioning of a "devil", then the other may be called the functioning of a "Buddha". As long as the Buddha function—the human capability for inventiveness imbued with compassion—exists, then a way can be found to abolish nuclear weapons. This was Mr. Toda's conviction.

Today's "Festival of Youth" has been blessed with clear, sunny skies free of any trace of yesterday's storm, as if the heavens themselves have responded to your enthusiasm. With a great feeling of joy, I watched the competitors among you display the Soka Gakkai spirit in each event, as the rest of you wholeheartedly applauded their efforts.

Nevertheless, for all the joy I feel today, it is inevitable that the Soka Gakkai will encounter persecution again. I am also fully prepared to meet any attack that comes my way personally. Having said that, I would now like to share with you what I hope you will regard as the first of my final instructions for the future.

As I have long said, the responsibility for the coming era will be shouldered by the youth. There is no need for me to tell you that *kosen-rufu* [spreading the value of respect for life] is our mission. We must absolutely achieve it. But today I would like to state clearly my feelings and attitude regarding the testing of nuclear weapons, a topic that is now being debated heatedly in society. I hope that, as my disciples, you will inherit the declaration I am about to make today and, to the best of your ability, spread its intent throughout the world.

Although a movement to ban the testing of nuclear weapons is now underway around the world, it is my wish to attack the problem at its root, that is, to rip out the claws that are hidden in the very depths of this issue. Thus I advocate that those who venture to use nuclear weapons, irrespective of their nationality or whether their country is victorious or defeated, be sentenced to death without exception.

Why do I say this? Because we, the citizens of the world, have an inviolable right to live. Anyone who tries to jeopardize this right is a devil incarnate, a fiend, a monster. I propose that humankind applies, in every case, the death penalty to anyone responsible for using nuclear weapons, even if that person is on the winning side.

Even if a country should conquer the world through the use of nuclear weapons, the conquerors must be viewed as devils, as evil incarnate. I believe that it is the mission of every member of the youth division in Japan to disseminate this idea throughout the globe.

I shall end by expressing my eager expectation for you to spread this first appeal of mine to the entire world with the powerful spirit you have shown in today's sports festival.

APPENDIX 2

The Russell–Einstein Manifesto

The declaration published here was first announced on July 9, 1955 in London. The British philosopher Lord Bertrand Russell, the American theoretical physicist Albert Einstein, and Dr. (later Professor) Joseph Rotblat, were among the eleven eminent scientists from around the world who signed it. The declaration aimed at abolishing nuclear weapons and, furthermore, abolishing war itself as a means to solve whatever disputes might arise from differences in ideologies or race or other problems besetting the world. It urged the human race to seek peaceful means of resolving conflict.

Only three months before the declaration was made public, Professor Einstein passed away. Thus, the Russell–Einstein Declaration is also considered Professor Einstein's last will and testament for humanity. As the practical embodiment of the message contained within this declaration, the first of the Pugwash Conference was held in 1957.

In the tragic situation which confronts humanity, we feel that scientists should assemble in conference to appraise the perils that have arisen as a result of the development of weapons of mass destruction, and to discuss a resolution in the spirit of the appended draft.

We are speaking on this occasion, not as members of this or that nation, continent, or creed, but as human beings, members of the species Man, whose continued existence is in doubt. The world is full of conflicts; and, overshadowing all minor conflicts, the titanic struggle between Communism and anti-Communism.

Almost everybody who is politically conscious has strong feelings about one or more of these issues; but we want you, if you can, to set aside such feelings and consider yourselves only as members of a biological species which has had a remarkable history, and whose disappearance none of us can desire.

We shall try to say no single word which should appeal to one group rather than to another. All, equally, are in peril, and, if the peril is understood, there is hope that they may collectively avert it.

We have to learn to think in a new way. We have to learn to ask ourselves, not what steps can be taken to give military victory to whatever group we prefer, for there no longer are such steps; the question we have to ask ourselves is: what steps can be taken to prevent a military contest of which the issue must be disastrous to all parties?

The general public, and even many men in positions of authority, have not realized what would be involved in a war with nuclear bombs. The general public still thinks in terms of the obliteration of cities. It is understood that the new bombs are more powerful than the old, and that, while one A-bomb could obliterate Hiroshima, one H-bomb could obliterate the largest cities, such as London, New York, and Moscow.

No doubt in an H-bomb war great cities would be obliterated. But this is one of the minor disasters that would have to be faced. If everybody in London, New York, and Moscow were exterminated, the world might, in the course of a few centuries, recover from the blow. But we now know, especially since the Bikini test, that nuclear bombs can gradually spread destruction over a very much wider area than had been supposed.

It is stated on very good authority that a bomb can now be manufactured which will be 2,500 times as powerful as that which destroyed Hiroshima. Such a bomb, if exploded near the ground or under water, sends radio-active particles into the upper air. They sink gradually and reach the surface of the earth in the form of a deadly dust or rain. It was this dust which infected the Japanese fishermen and their catch of fish. No one knows how widely such lethal radio-active particles might be diffused, but the best authorities are unanimous in saying that a war with H-bombs might possibly put an end to the human race. It is feared that if many H-bombs are used there will be universal death, sudden only for a minority, but for the majority a slow torture of disease and disintegration.

Many warnings have been uttered by eminent men of science and by authorities in military strategy. None of them will say that the worst results are certain. What they do say is that these results are possible, and no one can be sure that they will not be realized. We have not yet found that the views of experts on this question depend in any degree upon their politics or prejudices. They depend only, so far as our researches have revealed, upon the extent of the particular expert's knowledge. We have found that the men who know most are the most gloomy.

Here, then, is the problem which we present to you, stark and dreadful and inescapable: Shall we put an end to the human race; or shall mankind renounce war? People will not face this alternative because it is so difficult to abolish war.

The abolition of war will demand distasteful limitations of national sovereignty. But what perhaps impedes understanding of the situation more than anything else is that the term "mankind" feels vague and abstract. People scarcely realize in imagination that the danger is to themselves and their children and their grandchildren, and not only to a dimly apprehended humanity. They can scarcely bring themselves to grasp that they, individually, and those whom they love are in imminent danger of perishing agonizingly. And so they hope that perhaps war may be allowed to continue provided modern weapons are prohibited.

This hope is illusory. Whatever agreements not to use H-bombs had been reached in time of peace, they would no longer be considered binding in time of war, and both sides would set to work to manufacture H-bombs as soon as war broke out, for, if one side manufactured the bombs and the other did not, the side that manufactured them would inevitably be victorious.

Although an agreement to renounce nuclear weapons as part of a general reduction of armaments would not afford an ultimate solution, it would serve certain important purposes. First, any agreement between East and West is to the good in so far as it tends to diminish tension. Second, the abolition of thermo-nuclear weapons, if each side believed that the other had carried it out sincerely, would lessen the fear of a sudden attack in the style of Pearl Harbour, which at present keeps both sides in a state of nervous apprehension. We should, therefore, welcome such an agreement though only as a first step.

Most of us are not neutral in feeling, but, as human beings, we have to remember that, if the issues between East and West are to be decided in any manner that can give any possible satisfaction to anybody, whether Communist or anti-Communist, whether Asian or European or American, whether White or Black, then these issues must not be decided by war. We should wish this to be understood, both in the East and in the West.

There lies before us, if we choose, continual progress in happiness, knowledge, and wisdom. Shall we, instead, choose death, because we cannot forget our quarrels? We appeal as human beings to human beings: Remember your humanity, and forget the rest. If you can do so, the way lies open to a new Paradise; if you cannot, there lies before you the risk of universal death.

Resolution:

WE invite this Congress, and through it the scientists of the world and the general public, to subscribe to the following resolution:

"In view of the fact that in any future world war nuclear weapons will certainly be employed, and that such weapons threaten the continued existence of mankind, we urge the governments of the world to realize, and to acknowledge publicly, that their purpose cannot be furthered by a world war, and we urge them, consequently, to find peaceful means for the settlement of all matters of dispute between them."

Max Born
Percy W. Bridgman
Albert Einstein
Leopold Infeld
Frederic Joliot-Curie
Herman J. Muller
Linus Pauling
Cecil F. Powell
Joseph Rotblat
Bertrand Russell
Hideki Yukawa

Appendix 3

The Nobel Lecture

Given by Professor Joseph Rotblat

The manuscript that follows is of the lecture given by Professor Joseph Rotblat in acceptance of the Nobel Peace Prize at ceremonies held in Oslo, Norway, on December 10, 1995. In his lecture, he points to the idea of maintaining an arsenal of nuclear weapons as a deterrent, a concept cherished since the start of the East–West Cold War by nations possessing nuclear weapons, as the very factor multiplying the danger to humanity. Now is the time for those nations that possess such weaponry to step forward and abolish nuclear weaponry, he urged. He called on scientists themselves to acknowledge their role and also their responsibility. In order to build a world without war as humanity's duty to the human race, he appealed to all people in all walks of life to join hands in order to accomplish the task.

Remember Your Humanity

At this momentous event in my life—the acceptance of the Nobel Peace Prize—I want to speak as a scientist, but also as a human being. From my earliest days I had a passion for science. But science, the exercise of the supreme power of the human intellect, was always linked in my mind with benefit to people. I saw science as being in harmony with humanity. I did not imagine that the second half of my life would be spent on efforts to avert a mortal danger to humanity created by science.

The practical release of nuclear energy was the outcome of many years of experimental and theoretical research. It had great potential for the common good. But the first the general public learned about the discovery was the news of the destruction of Hiroshima by the atom bomb. A splendid achievement of science and technology had turned malign. Science became identified with death and destruction.

It is painful to me to admit that this depiction of science was deserved. The decision to use the atom bomb on Japanese cities, and the consequent buildup of enormous nuclear arsenals, was made by governments, on the basis of political and military perceptions. But scientists on both sides of the iron curtain played a very significant role in maintaining the momentum of the nuclear arms race throughout the four decades of the Cold War.

The role of scientists in the nuclear arms race was expressed bluntly by Lord Zuckerman, for many years Chief Scientific Adviser to the British Government:[1]

> When it comes to nuclear weapons ... it is the man in the laboratory who at the start proposes that for this or that arcane reason it would be useful to improve an old or to devise a new nuclear warhead. It is he, the technician, not the commander in the field, who is at the heart of the arms race.

Long before the terrifying potential of the arms race was recognized, there was a widespread instinctive abhorrence of nuclear weapons, and a strong desire to get rid of them. Indeed, the very first resolution of the General Assembly of the United Nations—adopted unanimously—called for the elimination of nuclear weapons. But the world was then polarized by the bitter ideological struggle between East and West. There was no chance to meet this call. The chief task was to stop the arms race before it brought utter disaster. However, after the collapse of communism and the disintegration of the Soviet Union, any rationale for having nuclear weapons disappeared. The quest for their total elimination could be resumed. But the nuclear powers still cling tenaciously to their weapons.

Let me remind you that nuclear disarmament is not just an ardent desire of the people, as expressed in many resolutions of the United Nations. It is a legal commitment by the five official nuclear states, entered into when they signed the Non-Proliferation Treaty. Only a few months ago, when the indefinite extension of the Treaty was agreed, the nuclear powers committed themselves again to complete nuclear disarmament. This is still their declared goal. But the declarations are not matched by their policies, and this divergence seems to be intrinsic.

Since the end of the Cold War two main nuclear powers have begun to make big reductions in their nuclear arsenals. Each of them is dismantling about 2,000 nuclear warheads a year. If this program continued, all nuclear warheads could be dismantled in little over ten years from now. We have the technical means to create a nuclear-weapon-free world in about a decade. Alas, the present program does not provide for this. When the START 2 treaty has been implemented—and remember it has not yet been ratified—we will be left with some 15,000 nuclear warheads, active and in reserve. Fifteen thousand weapons with an average yield of twenty Hiroshima bombs.

Unless there is a change in the basic philosophy, we will not see a reduction of nuclear arsenals to zero for a very long time, if ever. The present basic philosophy is nuclear deterrence. This was stated clearly in the US Nuclear Posture Review which concluded: "Post-Cold War environment requires nuclear deterrence,"[2] and this is echoed by other nuclear states. Nuclear weapons are kept as a hedge against some unspecified dangers.

This policy is simply an inertial continuation from the Cold War era. The Cold War is over but Cold War thinking survives. Then, we were told that a world war was prevented by the existence of nuclear weapons. Now, we are told that nuclear weapons prevent all kinds of war. These are arguments that purport to prove a negative. I am reminded of a story told in my boyhood at the time when radio communication began.

Two wise men were arguing about the ancient civilization in their respective countries. One said: "my country has a long history of technological development: we have carried out deep excavations and found a wire, which shows that already in the old days we had the telegraph". The other man retorted: "we too made excavations; we dug much deeper than you and found … nothing, which proves that already in those days we had wireless communication!"

There is no direct evidence that nuclear weapons prevented a world war. Conversely, it is known that they nearly caused one. The most terrifying moment in my life was October 1962, during the Cuban Missile Crisis. I did not know all the facts—we have learned only recently how close we were to war—but I knew enough to make me tremble. The lives of millions of people were about to end abruptly; millions of others were to suffer a lingering death; much of our civilization was to be destroyed. It all hung on the decision of one man, Nikita Khrushchev: would he or would he not yield to the US ultimatum?[3] This is the reality of nuclear weapons: they may trigger a world war; a war which, unlike previous ones, destroys all of civilization.

As for the assertion that nuclear weapons prevent wars, how many more wars are needed to refute this argument? Tens of millions have died in the many wars that have taken place since 1945. In a number of them nuclear states were directly involved. In two they were actually defeated. Having nuclear weapons was of no use to them.

To sum up, there is no evidence that a world without nuclear weapons would be a dangerous world. On the contrary, it would be a safer world, as I will show later.

We are told that the possession of nuclear weapons—in some cases even the testing of these weapons—is essential for national security. But this argument can be made by other countries as well. If the militarily most powerful—and least threatened—states need nuclear weapons for their security, how can one deny such security to countries that are truly insecure? The present nuclear policy is a recipe for proliferation. It is a policy for disaster.

To prevent this disaster—for the sake of humanity—we must get rid of all nuclear weapons.

Achieving this goal will take time, but it will never happen unless we make a start. Some essential steps towards it can be taken now. Several studies, and a number of public statements by senior military and political personalities, testify that—except for disputes between the present nuclear states—all military conflicts, as well as threats to peace, can be dealt with using conventional weapons. This means that the only function of nuclear weapons, while they exist, is to deter a nuclear attack. All nuclear weapon states should now recognize that this is so, and declare—in treaty form— that they will never be the first to use nuclear weapons. This would open the way to the gradual, mutual reduction of nuclear arsenals, down to zero. It would also open the way for a Nuclear Weapons Convention. This would be universal—it would prohibit all possession of nuclear weapons.

We will need to work out the necessary verification system to safeguard the Convention. A Pugwash study produced suggestions on these matters.[4] The mechanisms for negotiating such a Convention already exist. Entering into negotiations does not commit the parties. There is no reason why they should not begin now. If not now, when?

So I ask the nuclear powers to abandon the out-of-date thinking of the Cold War period and take a fresh look. Above all, I appeal to them to bear in mind the long-term threat that nuclear weapons pose to humankind, and to begin action towards their elimination. Remember your duty to humanity.

My second appeal is to my fellow scientists. I described earlier the disgraceful role played by a few scientists, caricatured as "Dr. Strangeloves",[5] in fueling the arms race. They did great damage to the image of science.

On the other side there are the scientists, in Pugwash and other bodies, who devote much of their time and ingenuity to averting the dangers created by advances in science and technology. However, they embrace only a small part of the scientific community. I want to address the scientific community as a whole.

You are doing fundamental work, pushing forward the frontiers of knowledge, but often you do it without giving much thought to the impact of your work on society. Precepts such as "science is neutral" or "science has nothing to do with politics", still prevail. They are remnants of the ivory tower mentality, although the ivory tower was finally demolished by the Hiroshima bomb.

Here, for instance, is a question: Should any scientist work on the development of weapons of mass destruction? A clear "no" was the answer recently given by Hans Bethe. Professor Bethe, a Nobel laureate, is the most senior of the surviving members of the Manhattan Project.[6] On the occasion of the fiftieth anniversary of Hiroshima, he issued a statement that I will quote in full.

> As the Director of the Theoretical Division at Los Alamos, I participated at the most senior level in the World War II Manhattan Project that produced the first atomic weapons.
>
> Now, at age 88, I am one of the few remaining such senior persons alive. Looking back at the half century since that time, I feel the most intense relief that these weapons have not been used since World War II, mixed with the horror that tens of thousands of such weapons have been built since that time – one hundred times more than any of us at Los Alamos could ever have imagined.
>
> Today we are rightly in an era of disarmament and dismantlement of nuclear weapons. But in some countries nuclear weapons development still continues. Whether and when the various Nations of the World can agree to stop this is uncertain. But individual scientists can still influence this process by withholding their skills.
>
> Accordingly, I call on all scientists in all countries to cease and desist from work creating, developing, improving and manufacturing further nuclear weapons - and, for that matter, other weapons of potential mass destruction such as chemical and biological weapons.

If all scientists heeded this call there would be no more new nuclear warheads; no French scientists at Mururoa;[7] no new chemical and biological poisons. The arms race would be truly over.

But there are other areas of scientific research that may directly or indirectly lead to harm to society. This calls for constant vigilance. The purpose of some government or industrial research is sometimes concealed, and misleading information is presented to the public. It should be the duty of scientists to expose such malfeasance. "Whistle-blowing" should become part of the scientist's ethos. This may bring reprisals, a price to be paid for one's convictions. The price may be very heavy, as illustrated by the disproportionately severe punishment of Mordechai Vanunu.[8] I believe he has suffered enough.

The time has come to formulate guidelines for the ethical conduct of scientists, perhaps in the form of a voluntary Hippocratic Oath. This would be particularly valuable for young scientists when they embark on a scientific career. The US Student Pugwash Group has taken up this idea—and that is very heartening.

At a time when science plays such a powerful role in the life of society, when the destiny of the whole of mankind may hinge on the results of scientific research, it is incumbent on all scientists to be fully conscious of that role, and conduct themselves accordingly. I appeal to my fellow scientists to remember their responsibility to humanity.

My third appeal is to my fellow citizens in all countries: Help us to establish lasting peace in the world.

I have to bring to your notice a terrifying reality: with the development of nuclear weapons Man has acquired, for the first time in history, the technical means to destroy the whole of civilization in a single act. Indeed, the whole human species is endangered, by nuclear weapons or by other means of wholesale destruction which further advances in science are likely to produce.

I have argued that we must eliminate nuclear weapons. While this would remove the immediate threat, it will not provide permanent security. Nuclear weapons cannot be disinvented. The knowledge of how to make them cannot be erased. Even in a nuclear-weapon-free world, should any of the great powers become involved in a military confrontation, they would be tempted to rebuild their nuclear arsenals. That would still be a better situation than the one we have now, because the rebuilding would take a considerable time, and in that time the dispute might be settled. A nuclear-weapon-free world would be safer than the present one. But the danger of the ultimate catastrophe would still be there.

The only way to prevent it is to abolish war altogether. War must cease to be an admissible social institution. We must learn to resolve our disputes by means other than military confrontation.

This need was recognized forty years ago when we said in the Russell–Einstein Manifesto:

Here, then, is the problem which we present to you, stark and dreadful, and inescapable: Shall we put an end to the human race; or shall mankind renounce war?

The abolition of war is also the commitment of the nuclear weapon states: Article VI of the NPT calls for a treaty on general and complete disarmament under strict and effective international control.

Any international treaty entails some surrender of national sovereignty, and is generally unpopular. As we said in the Russell-Einstein Manifesto: "The abolition of war will demand distasteful limitations of national sovereignty." Whatever system of governance is eventually adopted, it is important that it carries the people with it. We need to convey the message that safeguarding our common property, humankind, will require developing in each of us a new loyalty: a loyalty to mankind. It calls for the nurturing of a feeling of belonging to the human race. We have to become world citizens.

Notwithstanding the fragmentation that has occurred since the end of the Cold War, and the many wars for recognition of national or ethnic identities, I believe that the prospects for the acceptance of this new loyalty are now better than at the time of the Russell–Einstein Manifesto. This is so largely because of the enormous progress made by science and technology during these forty years. The fantastic advances in communication and transportation have shrunk our globe. All nations of the world have become close neighbors. Modern information techniques enable us to learn instantly about every event in every part of the globe. We can talk to each other via the various networks. This facility will improve enormously with time, because the achievements so far have only scratched the surface. Technology is driving us together. In many ways we are becoming like one family.

In advocating the new loyalty to mankind I am not suggesting that we give up national loyalties. Each of us has loyalties to several groups—from the smallest, the family, to the largest, at present, the nation. Many of these groups provide protection for their members. With the global threats resulting from science and technology, the whole of humankind now needs protection. We have to extend our loyalty to the whole of the human race.

What we are advocating in Pugwash, a war-free world, will be seen by many as a Utopian dream. It is not Utopian. There already exist in the world large regions, for example, the European Union, within which war is inconceivable. What is needed is to extend these to cover the world's major powers.

In any case, we have no choice. The alternative is unacceptable. Let me quote the last passage of the Russell–Einstein Manifesto:

We appeal, as human beings, to human beings: Remember your humanity and forget the rest. If you can do so, the way lies open to a new Paradise; if you cannot, there lies before you the risk of universal death.

The quest for a war-free world has a basic purpose: survival. But if in the process we learn how to achieve it by love rather than by fear, by kindness rather than by compulsion; if in the process we learn to combine the essential with the enjoyable, the expedient with the benevolent, the practical with the beautiful, this will be an extra incentive to embark on this great task.

Above all, remember your humanity.

From Irwin Abrams, ed, *Nobel Lectures, Peace 1991–1995* (Singapore: World Scientific Publishing Co., 1999).

Glossary

Afghanistan conflict, Soviet army invaded Afghanistan in 1979 to bolster the communist government of Afghanistan and withdrew in 1989

Alexander the Great (356–323 BC), king of Macedon; conquered Syria, Egypt and Persia; created the Hellenistic cultural foundation

Amnesty International, a worldwide non-governmental organization to protect the human rights provided for in the Universal Declaration of Human Rights

Annan, Kofi (1938–), born in Ghana; the seventh secretary-general of the United Nations; awarded Nobel Peace Prize (2001)

Apartheid means "separateness" in Afrikaans; a system of racial segregation in South Africa (1948–1991)

Atomic bombs Hiroshima became the first civilian target of the atomic bomb on August 6, 1945; the second civilian population targeted was Nagasaki three days later; about 250,000 people were killed by the two bombs

Augustine (354–430), Roman theologian and philosopher, a bishop in the early Christian church, canonized as St. Augustine of Hippo

Auschwitz, a town in the south of Poland; site of a Nazi German concentration camp during World War II

Berlin Wall, a barrier built by East Germany in 1961 to separate West Berlin and East Berlin; a symbol of the Cold War, demolished in 1989

Bhagavad-Gita, an Indian religious document and one of the most important sacred writings for the Vishnu school of Hinduism

Bohr, Niels Henrik David (1885–1962), Danish physicist; made essential contributions to understanding atomic structure and attempted peaceful application of atomic energy

Boulding, Elise (1920–), Norwegian-American peace activist, wife of Kenneth Boulding, author of *Culture of Peace*

Chadwick, James (1891–1974), awarded Nobel Prize in Physics for his discovery of neutron (1935); participated in the Manhattan Project during World War II

Chemical Weapons Convention came into force in 1997; prohibits all development, production, acquisition, stockpiling, transfer, and use of chemical weapons; signed by 167 countries at the present time

Churchill, Winston Leonard Spencer- (1874-1965), Prime Minister of UK during World War II; awarded Nobel Prize in Literature (1953)

Cobalt, element in the periodic table that has the symbol Co and atomic number 27; component of vitamin B12; radioactive in the artificial isotope Co 60

Cold War, postwar period of ideological conflict between the US and the USSR involving confrontations short of full-scale war; abandoned in 1991

Comprehensive Nuclear Test Ban Treaty (CTBT) bans all nuclear explosions in all environments, whether for military or civilian purposes; adopted in 1996; 176 countries are signatories at the present time

Convention on the Prohibition of Anti-Personnel Mines entered into force in 1999; concluded for the purpose of abolishing all anti-personnel mines

Cousins, Norman (1915–1990), American essayist and *Saturday Review* editor

Cuban Missile Crisis, tense confrontation between the USSR and US over the USSR deployment of nuclear missiles in Cuba in 1962

Curie, Marie (1867–1934), born in Poland, chemist and pioneer of radiology

Cyclotron, accelerator in which atomic particles move in a spiral path under the influence of an alternating voltage and magnetic field

Daigo-Fukuryu-Maru, Japanese tuna fishing boat, exposed to and contaminated by nuclear fallout from the US's Castle Bravo thermonuclear device test on Bikini Atoll in 1954, resulting in twenty-three casualties and one fatality

Declaration Against Nuclear Weapons, address by Josei Toda, the second president of Soka Gakkai, at the Eastern Japan Youth Division Sports Meeting sponsored by Soka Gakkai at the Mitsuzawa Stadium, Yokohama, Kanagawa Prefecture, on September 8, 1957. See Appendix 1.

Deterrence theory, a defensive strategy developed after World War II and used throughout the Cold War in which nations develop and stockpile nuclear weapons so that other nations will not attack for fear of retaliation

Dresden, capital city of the German federal state of Saxony; known for the controversial firebombing by Allied air forces during World War II

Eaton, Cyrus Stephen (1883–1979), Canadian industrialist and politician; born in Pugwash, Nova Scotia; founded several steel, coal and railroad companies

Einstein, Albert (1879–1955), German-Swiss-US scientist, former patent examiner, theoretical physicist; noted for his Theory of Relativity and Special Theory of Relativity; advocate of nuclear disarmament; awarded Nobel Prize for Physics (1921)

Eisenhower, Dwight David (1890–1969), American soldier and politician; Supreme Commander of the Allied forces in Europe during World War II; thirty-fourth President of the US (1953–1961)

Erasmus, Desiderius (1466–1536), Dutch humanist and theologian; diffused Renaissance culture and knowledge to North Europe

Fermi, Enrico (1901–1954), Italian-American physicist, awarded Nobel Prize in Physics (1938); expert on the neutron; responsible for first controlled nuclear chain reaction in 1942

Frisch, Otto Robert (1904–1979), Austrian-British physicist; studied fission of uranium nucleus

Gandhi, Mohandas Karamchand, "Mahatma Gandhi" (1869–1948), leader of the Indian nationalist movement against British rule, esteemed for his doctrine of nonviolent protest

Global Compact, ten principles for the human rights, labor, etc. suggested by UN Secretary-General Kofi Annan to business leaders at the World Economic Forum in 1999

Gorbachev, Mikhail Sergeyevich (1931–), politician and the last president of the USSR; his political reforms led to the end of the Cold War and also the dissolution of USSR; awarded Nobel Peace Prize (1990)

Greenpeace, a politically and financially independent organization formed to stop environmental destruction

Groves, Leslie Richard (1896–1970), US army officer, technological and administrative leader of the Manhattan Project that developed atomic bombs during World War II

Hawking, Stephen William (1942–), British theoretical physicist, the Lucasian professor of mathematics at the University of Cambridge

Heavy hydrogen, also called deuterium; general term for the heavy isotope of hydrogen

Hiroshima Peace Memorial, called Genbaku Dome/the Atomic Bomb Dome; UNESCO World Heritage Site in Hiroshima, Japan; considered the ground zero of the first nuclear explosion on August 6, 1945

Hitler, Adolf (1889–1945), leader of the National Socialist German Workers' Party [Nazi Party], Chancellor of Germany from 1933; governed Germany absolutely as Führer [Leader] from 1934 to his death

Holocaust, systematic, state-sponsored killing of six million Jewish men, women and children by Nazi Germany and its collaborators during World War II

Human revolution, the process of self-development and self-realization accomplished through compassionate Buddhist activities; title of the fictionalized history of Soka Gakkai written by Daisaku Ikeda

Hungarian Uprising, an anti-Soviet revolt in Hungary in 1956; Soviet troops intruded and established a pro-Soviet Hungarian government

Hydrogen bombs, formerly known as thermonuclear bombs; nuclear fusion is used in bombs hundreds of times more powerful than fission weapons

Imphal, capital of Manipur, India; a World War II campaign in which the Japanese army attempted to capture the capital

Infeld, Leopold (1989–1968), Polish physicist; one of eleven signatories to the Russell–Einstein Manifesto in 1955

International Committee of the Red Cross, established in 1863; the origin of the International Red Cross and Red Crescent Movement; protects the lives and dignity of victims of war and internal violence and provides them with medical aid and food

International Court of Justice, the principal judicial organ of the United Nations in The Hague, Netherlands

International Physicians for the Prevention of Nuclear War (IPPNW), international physicians' organization dedicated to research, education and advocacy relevant to the prevention of nuclear war

Jaspers, Karl Theodor (1883–1969), German psychiatrist and philosopher

Kant, Immanuel (1724–1804), German philosopher and scientist; author of *Critique of Pure Reason*

Kennedy, John Fitzgerald (1917–1963), thirty-fifth President of the US (1961–1963); his administration faced challenges by events like the Cuban Missile Crisis, the building of the Berlin Wall and the Vietnam War

Khrushchev, Nikita (1894–1971), Soviet premier (1953–1964) whose policy was de-Stalinization and peaceful coexistence with capitalist countries

Korean War, a conflict between North Korea and South Korea (1950–1953); considered a proxy war between the US and its Western democratic allies and the Communist powers of China and the USSR

Kosygin, Aleksei (1904–1980), Soviet premier (1964–1980), known as a pragmatic economic administrator

Lawrence, Ernest Orlando (1901–1958), American physicist; invented the cyclotron; awarded Nobel Prize in Physics (1939)

Los Alamos National Laboratory, founded during World War II to coordinate the scientific research of the Manhattan Project toward developing nuclear weapons; first directed by Robert Oppenheimer

Makiguchi, Tsunesaburo (1871–1944), educator, founder-president of Soka Gakkai, and author of *Education for Creative Living* and *A Geography of Human Life*

Mandela, Nelson (1918–), a leader of African National Conference (ANC); first president of free and democratic South Africa; awarded Nobel Peace Prize (1993)

Manhattan Project, US World War II project to develop nuclear weapons; resulted in production and detonation of atomic bombs at Hiroshima and Nagasaki in 1945

McCarthy, Joseph Raymond (1908–1957), Republican member of US senate who conducted congressional investigations accusing innocent persons of communist affiliations

McNamara, Robert (1916–), American businessman and politician; a former US secretary of defense (1961–1968)

Meitner, Lise (1878–1968), Austrian physicist, studied radioactivity and nuclear physics; naturalized Swedish

Military–industrial complex, combination of the US armed forces, arms industry and associated political and commercial interests

Moscow State University, the largest and oldest university in Russia, founded in 1755 by M. V. Lomonosov

Mussolini, Benito Amilcare Andrea (1883–1945), Italian politician; created a fascist state in 1922 and promoted external invasion; made Italy a member of the Tripartite Pact

Mutually Assured Destruction (MAD), military strategy meant as a deterrent to nuclear war by assuring reciprocal attack and destruction by nuclear weapons

Nehru, Jawaharlal (1889–1964), Indian politician; studied in UK; disciple of Gandhi; a leader of India's independence struggle; the first Prime Minister of India (1947–1964)

Nichiren Daishonin (1222–1282), Japanese Buddhist prophet, founder of Nichiren Buddhism which reveres the teachings of the Lotus Sutra

Normandy campaign, 1944 landing on Normandy beaches [France] by US, UK and Canadian forces allied against Nazi Germany; led to the liberation of Paris and defeat of Nazi Germany in World War II

North Atlantic Treaty Organization (NATO), an international military organization for defense collaboration; established in 1949

Nuclear fission, splitting of the nucleus of heavy elements [uranium, plutonium, etc.] into particles in a chain reaction

Nuclear physics, branch of physics concerned with the nucleus of the atom, elementary particles and cosmic rays

Nucleus of an atom, dense region in an atom's center thought to consist of protons and neutrons

Ogawa, Iwao (1921–), Japanese nuclear physicist, lectured at Tokyo University and Rikkyo University

Oliphant, Mark (1901–2000), Australian physicist; responsible for the development of microwave radar; led nuclear fusion experiments resulting in the discovery of new forms of hydrogen (deuterium and tritium) in 1934; vigorous proponent of nuclear disarmament

Oppenheimer, Robert (1904–1967), American theoretical physicist; scientific director of the Manhattan Project, the first director of Los Alamos National Laboratory

Ortega y Gasset, José (1883–1955), Spanish philosopher who greatly influenced Spain's twentieth-century cultural and literary renaissance

Oxfam International, a confederation of twelve organizations working to find lasting solutions to poverty, suffering and injustice

Partial Test Ban Treaty (PTBT), bans all test explosions of nuclear weapons in the atmosphere, in outer space, and under water; first signed by the US, UK and USSR in 1963 in Moscow, with 108 signatory countries by the end of the year

Pascal, Blaise (1623–1962), French mathematician, physicist, and religious philosopher; author of *Pensées*

Pauling, Linus (1901–1994), noted for his studies on molecular structure and chemical bonding; an early advocate of the health benefits of megadoses of vitamin C; awarded the Nobel Prize for Chemistry (1954) and the Nobel Peace Prize (1962) for his efforts on behalf of nuclear weapons control

Peierls, Rudolf Ernst (1907–1995), German-British physicist, delivered paper on the energy of nuclear fission that triggered UK participation in the Manhattan Project

Peking University, one of the oldest and most prestigious universities in China, founded in 1898

Pugwash Conferences on Science and World Affairs, international organization of scholars and public figures founded in 1957 by Joseph Rotblat and Bertrand Russell in Pugwash, Canada, to reduce the danger of armed conflict and to seek solutions to global security; Pugwash and Rotblat jointly won Nobel Peace Prize in 1995 for efforts toward nuclear disarmament

Rapoport, Anatol (1911–), Russian-American mathematician and biologist; pioneer in studies of game theory in conflict resolution

Rees, Martin John (1942–), UK Astronomer Royal, Master of Trinity College, Cambridge since 2004

Rhodes, Richard (1937–), American author; awarded Pulitzer Prize for his *The Making of the Atomic Bomb*

Robespierre, Maximilien Marie Isidore de (1758–1794), French revolutionary, leader of the Jacobins, virtual dictator during France's Reign of Terror

Roosevelt, Franklin Delano (1882–1945), thirty-second President of the US (1933–1945), led the US through the Great Depression with his New Deal policies

Russell, Bertrand (1872–1970), British philosopher and mathematician; awarded Nobel Prize in Literature (1950); author of *Human Knowledge*

Russell–Einstein Manifesto, issued in London in 1955 by Bertrand Russell; signed by eleven preeminent intellectuals and scientists, including Albert Einstein; a call for world leaders to seek peaceful resolutions to international conflict. See Appendix 2

September 11 attacks, a series of coordinated suicide attacks upon the US carried out on September 11, 2001

Soka Gakkai, lay religious organization founded in Japan in 1930 and formally inaugurated in 1937; the society follows the teachings of Nichiren, based on the Lotus Sutra's philosophy of compassion

Stalin, Joseph (1879–1953), Soviet politician and dictator; noted for a policy of five-year plans that radically altered social structures and resulted in the deaths of millions

Suez Canal Crisis, the UK, France and Israel invaded Egypt when Egyptian President Gamal Abdel Nasser nationalized the canal in 1956

Szilárd, Leó (1898–1964), Hungarian-American physicist; worked on the Manhattan Project but opposed the atomic bombing in Hiroshima and Nagasaki

Tagore, Rabindranath (1861–1941), Bengali poet, writer, composer and painter; author of *Gitanjali*; awarded the Nobel Prize for Literature (1913)

Teller, Edward (1908–2003), Hungarian-American physicist; joined the Manhattan Project in 1942 and led development of the H-bomb

Toda Institute of Global Peace and Policy Research, founded in 1996 by Daisaku Ikeda; offices in Tokyo and Honolulu; sponsors research programs on global peace and human security policy issues

Toda, Josei (1900–1958), the second president of Soka Gakkai, a direct disciple of the founding president, Tsunesaburo Makiguchi, and mentor of the third president, Daisaku Ikeda

Tokugawa shogunate, government by hereditary military dictator; a time of peace, political stability and economic growth in Japan from 1603 to 1867

Tomonaga Shin'ichiro (1906–1979), Japanese physicist; influential in the development of quantum electro dynamics; awarded Nobel Prize in Physics (1965)

Treaty on the Non-Proliferation of Nuclear Weapons (NPT), entered into force in 1970; 189 signatory countries at present time

Tripartite Pact, also called the Three-Power Pact; signed in Berlin in 1940 by representatives of Nazi Germany, Fascist Italy and Japan to oppose the Allied forces of the UK, France and the US during World War II

Truman, Harry S. (1884–1972), thirty-third President of the USA (1945–1953); presided over termination of World War II and handling of postwar diplomatic issues

Urey, Harold Clayton (1893–1981), American chemist; proved the existence of the deuterium isotope of hydrogen in spectroscope experiments; awarded Nobel Prize in Chemistry (1934)

Verne, Jules Gabriel (1828–1905), French writer and pioneer of science-fiction genre, books include *Around the World in Eighty Days* and *Journey to the Moon*

Vietnam War, also Second Indochina War; conflict between North Vietnam and Viet Cong allies against South Vietnam and the US from 1960 to 1975

Warsaw Pact, international military organization of Socialist countries for defense collaboration; established in 1955

Yukawa, Hideki (1907–1981), Japanese physicist, awarded Nobel Prize for Physics (1949); signed the Russell–Einstein Manifesto in 1955

Notes

Chapter 1

1   Translated from Japanese: *Tomonaga Shin'ichiro Chosakushu* (The Collected Writings of Shin'ichiro Tomonaga) (Tokyo: Misuzu Shobo, 2001), vol. 5, pp. 67–68.
2   Linus Pauling and Daisaku Ikeda, *A Lifelong Quest for Peace* (Boston: Jones and Bartlett Publishers, 1992), p. 66.
3   *SGI Quarterly*, no. 31, January 2003, available at http://www.sgi.org/english/Features/quarterly/0301/portraits.htm.
4   J. Rotblat, J. Steinberger, D. Udgaonkari, eds, *A Nuclear-Weapon-Free World: Desirable? Feasible?*, 2nd edn, (Boulder, CO: Westview Press, 1996).

Chapter 3

1   Introduction to *Fighting for Peace* (Berkley: Creative Arts Book Company, 2004), p. ix.

Chapter 6

1   Arnold J. Toynbee and Daisaku Ikeda, *Choose Life* (Oxford: Oxford University Press, 1976), p. 191.
2   Ibid., p. 191.
3   Karl Jaspers, *Kleine Schule Des Philosophischen Denkens* (Philosophy Is for Everyone: A Short Course in Philosophical Thinking), (Munich: R. Piper, 1965), p. 174.

Chapter 7

1   Translated from Japanese: *The Mainichi Newspapers*, January 26, 1998, p. 3.
2   Robert S. McNamara, *Argument Without End* (New York: Public Affairs, 1999), p. 11.
3   Mikhail Gorbachev and Daisaku Ikeda, *Moral Lessons of the Twentieth Century* (London: I.B.Tauris, 2005), p. 52.

4   Saint Augustine, *The City of God Against the Pagans*, vol. II, books IV–VII, trans. William M. Green (Cambridge, MA: Harvard University Press, 1963), p. 17.
5   J. Rotblat, J. Steinberger, D. Udgaonkari, eds, *A Nuclear-Weapon-Free World: Desirable? Feasible?*, 2nd edn, (Boulder, CO: Westview Press, 1996), first published 1993.
6   Blaise Pascal, *Pensées*, translated by W. F. Trotter (London: J.M. Dent & Sons Ltd., 1947) , no. 298, p. 85.
7   Rabindranath Tagore, *The Spirit of Japan* (Tokyo: Indo-Japanese Association, 1916), p. 2.

Chapter 8

1   José Ortega y Gasset, *La rebelión de las masas* (Madrid: Revista de Occidente, 1929), p. 159.
2   Tsunesaburo Makiguchi, *A Geography of Human Life*, edited by Dayle M. Bethel (San Francisco: Caddo Gap Press, 2002), p. 11.
3   *Nichiren Daishonin Gosho Zenshu* (Collected Writings of Nichiren Daishonin) (Tokyo: Soka Gakkai, 1952), p. 1598.
4   Ibid., p. 258.
5   Desiderius Erasmus, *The Education of a Christian Prince*, translated by Lester K. Born (New York: Octagon Books, 1965), p. 213.

Chapter 9

1   *The Writings of Nichiren Daishonin*, translated by Soka Gakkai (Tokyo: Soka Gakkai, 1999), p. 998.
2   *The Record of the Orally Transmitted Teachings*, translated by Burton Watson (Tokyo: Soka Gakkai, 2004), p. 115.
3   *The Writings of Nichiren Daishonin*, translated by Soka Gakkai (Tokyo: Soka Gakkai, 1999), p. 536.
4   Stephen W. Hawking, *A Brief History of Time*, introduction by Carl Sagan (Toronto and New York, Bantam Books, 1988).
5   Stephen W. Hawking, *The Universe in a Nutshell* (New York: Bantam Books, 2001).
6   For example, Martin Rees, *Before the Beginning: Our Universe and Others* (New York: Basic Books, 1998).
7   Richard Rhodes, *The Making of the Atomic Bomb* (New York: Simon & Schuster, 1986), and Richard Rhodes, *Dark Sun: The Making of the Hydrogen Bomb* (New York: Simon & Schuster, 1996).
8   Daisaku Ikeda, *Fighting for Peace* (Berkley: Creative Arts Book Company, 2004), p. ix.

Chapter 10

1 September 21, 2004, New York.
2 *Hansard*, November 11, 1947.
3 September 25, 1961, New York.
4 Arnold J. Toynbee, *A Study of History* (London: Oxford University Press, 1951–1961), 12 vols.
5 Anatol Rapoport, *Decision Theory and Decision Behaviour* (Houndmills: Palgrave, 1997).
6 Bertrand Russell, *Has Man a Future?* (Baltimore: Penguin Books, 1964), p. 87.

Appendix 3

1 Baron Solly Zuckerman of Burnham Thorpe, Norfolk, held a number of such governmental appointments during World War II and after.
2 More recently, in the Pugwash Newsletter of October 1998 Rotblat refers to a recently leaked secret Presidential Decision Directive outlining nuclear strategy, which requires the retention of nuclear weapons for the foreseeable future as a basis for the national security of the United States.
3 In 1962 the Soviet Union moved to install nuclear missiles in Cuba in order to deter any attack on Cuba by the United States. The United States demanded that the missiles be withdrawn, and both the United States and the Soviet Union were on the brink of a nuclear war. However, Nikita Khrushchev, Soviet premier and first secretary of the Communist Party, agreed to withdraw the missiles, and the crisis passed.
4 Rotblat refers to the Pugwash volume, *Verification: Monitoring Disarmament* (1991), [*Verification: Monitoring Disarmament* (Pugwash Monograph), edited by Francesco Calogero, Marvin L. Goldberger and Sergei P. Kapitza (Boulder, CO: Westview Press, 1991)] written and edited by high caliber experts from both the West and the Soviet Union, which illustrates how Pugwash scientists of different ideological backgrounds could cooperate in approaching a sensitive security issue.
5 The 1964 black comedy anti-war film about the dropping of the bomb was entitled *Dr. Strangelove, or: How I Stopped Worrying and Learned to Love the Bomb*.
6 Hans Albrecht Bethe, born in Germany in 1906, resettled in the United States in 1935 to teach at Cornell University. He was at Los Alamos from 1943–46, and in 1958 he was scientific adviser to the United States at the nuclear test ban talks in Geneva. In 1967 he was awarded the Nobel Prize in Physics "for his contributions to the theory of nuclear reactions, especially his discoveries concerning the energy production in stars."

7   The South Pacific atoll of Mururoa in French Polynesia was the site of a series of French underwater nuclear bomb tests, which began in 1995 and ended in January 1996.

8   An Israeli technician, working at the Demona nuclear reactor, felt that Israel's secret production of plutonium there for nuclear weapons should be known by Israelis and the world, and as a matter of conscience he made the information public in 1985. He was lured to Rome by Israeli secret agents, kidnapped and brought back to Israel where he was secretly tried, convicted, and sentenced to eighteen years in prison. He spent at least the first twelve years in solitary confinement, while a worldwide campaign continued for his liberation. Adopted as a prisoner of conscience by Amnesty International, he has often been nominated for the Nobel Peace Prize.

Index